THE BEST ROUTES ON
BRITAIN'S MOUNTAINS

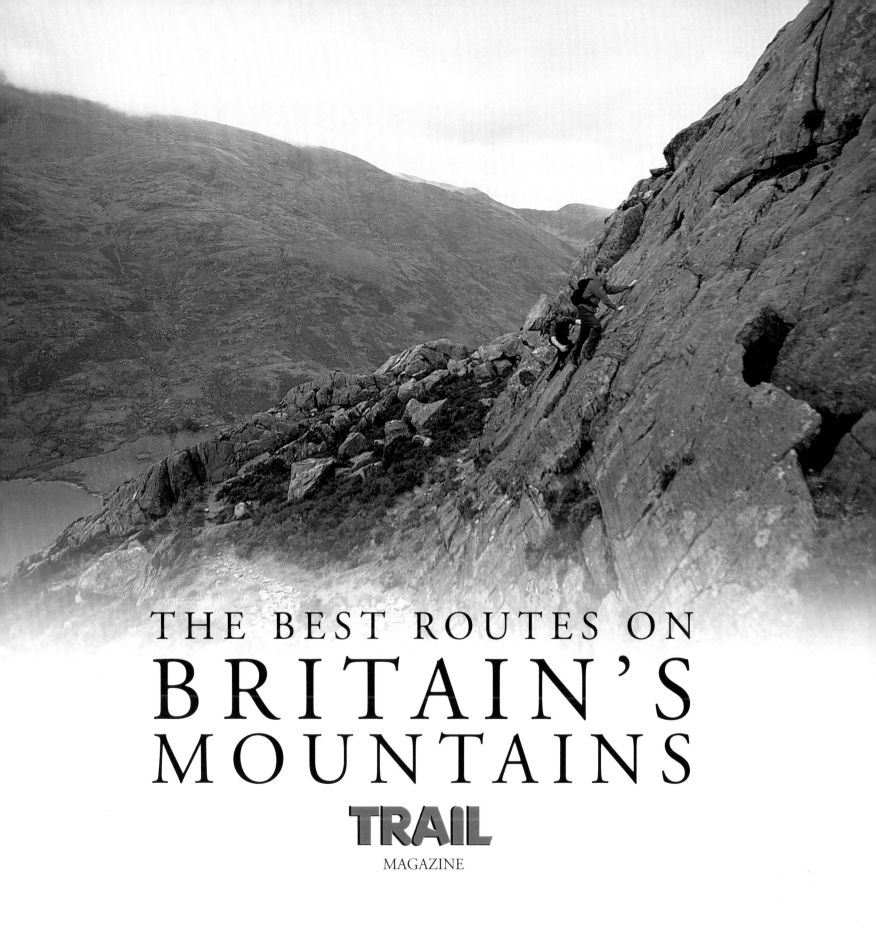

THE BEST ROUTES ON
BRITAIN'S
MOUNTAINS

TRAIL

MAGAZINE

First published in 2003

A catalogue record for this book is available from the British Library

ISBN 1 84425 144 6

Published jointly by
Haynes Publishing, Sparkford,
Yeovil, Somerset BA22 7JJ, England
Phone 01963 440635, www.haynes.co.uk
And
Emap Active Limited,
Wentworth House, Wentworth Street,
Peterborough PE1 1DS, England
Phone 01733 213700, www.emap.com

Printed and bound in England by J.H. Haynes & Co. Ltd, Sparkford

CONTENTS

We would like to acknowledge the illustration talent of Jeremy Ashcroft appearing throughout this book.

Beloved of bards and botanists, this 'violet' hill has a violent past.

Foreword
by Guy Procter
Britain's best mountain routes

They may not be the highest, but Britain's mountains offer some of the best walking in the world. Not just the big names like Snowdon, Ben Nevis, Helvellyn and Scafell Pike, whose names will be familiar to any tourist, but the lesser-known peaks and those cloaked in unpronounceability. An Teallach, Y Lliwedd, Sgurr Fhuaran, Ben Cruachan - their bristling syllables belong in the world of Tolkien, and if you're to make your way in this terra incognita, you need a reliable guide. Which is where this book comes in. Sourced from Trail magazine's experts, we've walked, mapped and assessed every major peak in the country. A generous selection of the best appears here. What you'll find is all the information you need to pick the route that's right for you. Each aims for the summit, but the menu of sights you'll see, and terrain you'll cross varies from route to route. Some are popular classics, some less frequented; some placid and gradual, some steep and demanding - whichever way you choose you'll bag a trophy mountain, and a guaranteed memorable day in the hills. Got a favourite mountain already? Our comprehensive mountain guides will help you get to know it better. Just starting out? Trust our informative fact files to pick ideal routes for beginners. Whatever you're looking for in the hills, the British mountains have it in spades. From the Lake District, where the hills are close-packed like a punnet of strawberries, to the Highlands, where the whole pick-your-own farm spreads out before you, there's a feast of fell-walking out there. Think of this book as your gourmet guide.

LOCATION	LAKE DISTRICT
HEIGHT	977m (3,206ft)
SUMMIT GR	NY215072

Scafell Pike

IT WINS NO PRIZES IN THE GLAMOUR STAKES, BUT THIS IS A MOUNTAIN
THAT SETS PULSES RACING AT THE MERE MENTION OF ITS NAME.

Words Jane Baker

Who's the daddy?!
Scafell and Scafell Pike
seen across Eskdale from
Esk Pike.
IAN EVANS/MOUNTAIN IMAGES

S cafell Pike struggled long and hard to gain the recognition it deserves. Slap bang in the middle of some of Lakeland's biggest hitters – Scafell, Great End, Great Gable and Bow Fell – its status as England's highest peak was overlooked for generations.

Being in such an inaccessible location didn't help matters, so it's no surprise that another notable peak over 3,000ft, Skiddaw, should have held the crown for so long. In fact, it wasn't until the 1820s that advances in mathematics and mapping finally saw the young pretender overthrown in what was a relatively bloodless coup.

But Scafell Pike was still not the obvious successor. Thanks to a natty optical illusion, the title of Nation's Biggest Peak went to its visually more impressive sibling Scafell. It took quite some time to realise that our affections were misplaced by a full 13m, and the crown finally took its rightful place on Scafell Pike's bald, weather-worn pate. You see, this isn't the most attractive of mountains. It seems that even the origins of its name were intended to poke fun at Blighty's behemoth. It's derived from two old Norse words *skalli* and *fjall* which means 'the fell with the bare summit'. Scafell Pike was know by local marauding Vikings as Skalli (which means 'Old Baldy' for those of you not familiar with Ancient Norse). As if all that looting and pillaging wasn't bad enough, they come over here and mock our mountains. Well really!

While neighbouring Scafell has taxing ascents up Lord's Rake and Broad Stand, plus some of the most famous rock-climbing cliffs in Britain, Scafell Pike is rather lacking in sheer mountain fun. But it's a suitably impressive peak nonetheless. It's grand, rocky and domed, and an essential tick on anyone's list. In fact, it's ideally placed for any walker who wants to get to the very heart of the Lake District.

Like the spokes in a wheel, the valleys of Wasdale, Borrowdale, Eskdale and Langdale radiate out from Scafell Pike – and this is an area where the boot really is king. It actually takes as long to drive around the range as it does to walk across it. There are various high-level walking routes up onto the summit to choose from, depending on what type of experience you want. The shortest follows the course of Lingmell Beck up to the great rocky mass of Brown Tongue, which is a fairly relentless trudge. As with all the routes onto Scafell Pike, you are continually rewarded with spectacular views, which open out before you like the pages of a great book. If it's scrambling you're after, head for Ill Crag or pick a line up the north-western slopes via Piers Gill and the crags of Round How and Broad Crag. And in winter, Great End is one of the most reliable crags for climbing in snow and ice conditions. As soon as the thermometer dips below zero it pulls on its thick ice layers and positively warms to the touch of crampons and ropes.

Scafell Pike may be visible from virtually every angle within the county of Cumbria, but paradoxically it's one of the most difficult mountains to get to and is notorious for causing navigational nightmares. If the weather turns bad and throws its gloomy cloak across the summit, getting back down without a map and compass can be very difficult. With the rush of adrenaline that hits them as they take that last step up onto England's highest point, walkers can easily lose their bearings. There are no easily distinguishable routes leading back off the summit, and many a soul has come down the mountain on a path they didn't intend to take, only to realise their car was parked over 30 miles away.

For Malcolm Guyatt of the National Parks Authority, Scafell Pike is quintessentially English – a distillation of what this country is all about. "On a clear day you can see the Pennines, south Lancashire and Morecambe Bay, the Isle of Man, Ireland and southern Scotland," explains Malcolm. "It's a place from where you can see why in times of war England is worth fighting for."

It is perhaps fitting, then, that the summit of Scafell Pike was bequeathed to the people of the Lake District as a war memorial. In 1920, the 3rd Lord Leconfield gave it to be a lasting monument to those who fell in World War One.

the routes

● The times given are for the walk to the summit only – not there and back.

1 CAM SPOUT ROUTE

Easy scramble by the spectacular Cam Spout Force accessed from Upper Eskdale via the Great Moss.

Start Brotherilkeld (**NY212012**)
Distance 8km (5 miles)
Time 3 hours
Height gain 884m
Terrain long valley, boggy moss, rocky ghyll, scree and rocky summit
Difficulty strenuous
Popularity quiet

Route Follow the lane and then either of the paths alongside the River Esk NE to Lingcove Bridge. Head N to Scar Lathing then W onto the Great Moss which is crossed to the foot of Cam Spout Force. Climb the rocks on the E side of the waterfall, continuing up the ghyll to Mickledore. At the stretcher box turn R and follow the rough path NE to Scafell Pike.

Lingmell (left), Scafell and Scafell Pike with the dip of the Mickledore linking the two.

JULIE FRYER

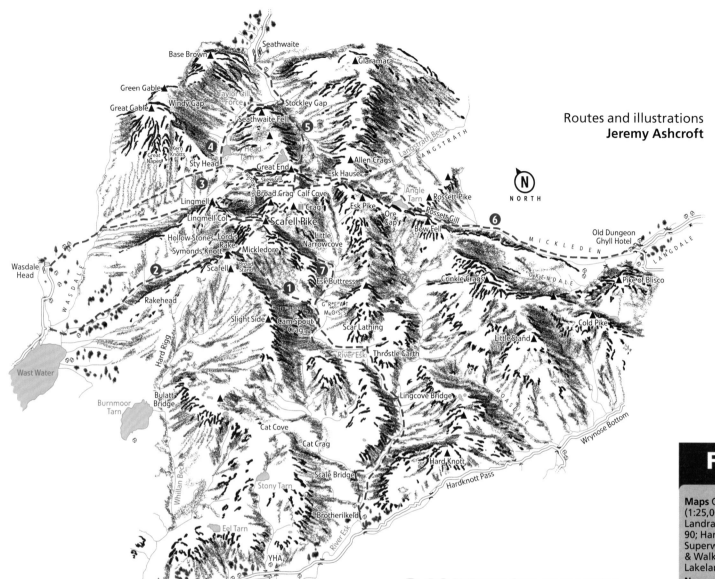

Routes and illustrations
Jeremy Ashcroft

2 BROWN TONGUE ROUTE

Climbs the steep, unremitting moraine of Brown Tongue – hard work, but a fine route with ever-expanding views of Pikes Crag and Scafell Crag.

Start National Trust Camp Site, Wasdale Head (**NY181076**)
Distance 4km (2½ miles)
Time 2½ hours
Height gain 913m
Terrain ghyll, steep moraine, boulders, scree and rocky summit
Difficulty strenuous
Popularity moderate

Route Take the permissive path past Brackenclose then cross the Lingmell Beck footbridge. On the other side follow the path E alongside the beck to a ford. Cross the ford and climb the steep path up Brown Tongue to Hollow Stones. Head SE up the steep scree to Mickledore. Turn L at the stretcher box and follow the rough path NE to Scafell Pike.

3 CORRIDOR ROUTE

Traverses the NW side of the main Scafell Pike ridge from Sty Head to Lingmell Col. A really splendid route taking in some of England's finest mountain scenery.

Start Wasdale Head (**NY186088**)
Distance 6km (3¾ miles)
Time 3 hours
Height gain 913m
Terrain steep-sided valley, scree path, rough craggy fellside, scree and rocky summit
Difficulty strenuous
Popularity moderate
Variation Can also be started from Seathwaite.
Sty Head is gained via the Stockley Bridge bridleway.

Route From Wasdale Head follow the bridleway that traverses E across the S face of Great Gable to Sty Head. Turn E at the stretcher box and follow the bridleway a short distance to a fork. Take the R branch and descend onto the Corridor Route which is followed as it climbs steadily SSW to Lingmell Col. Turn L and follow the rough path over scree and boulders SE to Scafell Pike.

4 SKEW GILL

An adventurous approach to the main Scafell Pike massif. Skew Gill, which holds one steep section, gives access to the impressive depths of Cust's Gully capped with it famous chock stone.

Start Seathwaite (**NY235121**)
Distance 7.6km (4¾ miles)
Time 3 hours
Height gain 921m
Terrain valley, rocky ghyll, gullies, rough mountain ridge and rocky summit
Difficulty strenuous (Grade 1 and Grade 2 scrambles/Grade 1 winter climb)
Popularity quiet

Route Take the bridleway S to Stockley Bridge, cross it and climb the steep zigzags W then head SW alongside Styhead Gill to Styhead Tarn. Turn E at a fork. Take the R branch and descend onto the Corridor Route which is followed to Skew Gill. Climb SE up the bed of Skew Gill to the steeper section which is passed on the L and continue to the col. Cross it and descend across Great End Crag to the bottom of Cust's Gully which is climbed direct onto Great End. Descend SE to the head of Calf Cove then join the main ridge path past Ill Crag and Broad Crag to Scafell Pike.

5 GRAINS GILL

Direct route from Borrowdale to the north end of the Scafell massif via Esk Hause.

Start Seathwaite (**NY235121**)
Distance 6.4km (4 miles)
Time 2½ hours
Height gain 889m
Terrain steep-sided valley, exposed col, stony cove, rough mountain ridge and rocky summit
Difficulty intermediate
Popularity moderate

Route Take the bridleway S past Stockley Bridge then L up Grains Gill to join the Esk Hause bridleway, turn L and follow it to the shelter near Esk Hause. Turn R and take the path W over Esk Hause and up through Calf Cove. At the top of the cove turn SW and follow the path past Ill Crag and Broad Crag to Scafell Pike.

6 FROM LANGDALE VIA ROSSETT GILL

A long but logical route taking in some exceptional mountain scenery.

Start Old Dungeon Ghyll Hotel, Langdale (**NY285061**)
Distance 8.9km (5½ miles)
Time 3½-4 hours
Height gain 1011m
Terrain long valley, steep fellside, rough mountain ridge and rocky summit
Difficulty strenuous
Popularity moderate

Route Follow the bridleway the length of Mickleden to a fork after a footbridge. Take the L branch as it climbs the zigzags alongside Rossett Gill W then NW to Angle Tarn. Pass the tarn and continue NW to the shelter near Esk Hause. Turn L and take the path W over Esk Hause up through Calf Cove. At the top of the cove head SW and follow the path past Ill Crag and Broad Crag to Scafell Pike.

7 LITTLE NARROWCOVE

Remote and wild, Little Narrowcove provides a fine route to Scafell Pike. It is reached by an approach along Upper Eskdale and a traverse across the bogs of the Great Moss.

Start Brotherilkeld (**NY212012**)
Distance 8.9km (5½ miles)
Time 3 hours
Height gain 884m
Terrain long valley, boggy moss, rocky ghyll, scree and rocky summit
Difficulty strenuous
Popularity quiet

Route Follow the lane then either of the paths by the River Esk NE to Lingcove Bridge. Head N to Scar Lathing veering W onto the Great Moss. Head N to an old wall and follow it by the River Esk past Esk Buttress to where the beck from Little Narrowcove enters the river. Ford the Esk and climb the fellside on the SW side of the beck to a shallow gully which is followed NW into Little Narrowcove proper. Continue NW up through the cove to the col, then turn L and climb the rocky path SW to Scafell Pike.

IAN EVANS/MOUNTAIN IMAGES

David Bethune Selkirk

My son Iain was 11 and I must have been 37 when we set off to climb Scafell and Scafell Pike. It is hard work coaxing an 11-year-old up the steep slopes of Lingmell from Wasdale on a hot day, but we made steady progress, pausing frequently to admire the view. I stopped to rearrange my rucksack and in no time Iain was about 200m ahead of me. I strode out to catch him up; but, no matter how I tried, he stayed ahead! He had the summit in his sights and was determined to be first to the top – the first time he had been above the 3,000ft mark since I had lugged him up Stuchd an Lochain in a baby rucksack.

Now the 11-year-old is 19 [see above], and I am also a few years older. Maybe I can't catch up with him on the hills any more, but I still lead him 150 to 22 in our Munro tallies! Will he overtake me again? I doubt it, but consult www.dbethune.com/mountains to see if I can stay ahead!

Jim Rowley
Gloucester

Torrential rain reduced the visibility to a few paces as I headed up Scafell Pike. Having met no-one for hours, I reached the summit thinking I was the last soul on earth. Suddenly two figures lurched out of the mist, shouting unintelligibly. One grabbed my shoulder and the other my hand. I couldn't believe it – at the highest point in England I was being mugged!

My hand was shaken vigorously and the blow on my shoulder turned into a hug – not the modus operandi of your average assailant. It transpired that I had encountered a pair of Dutch walkers who were completely lost. The weather had taken a turn for the worse and they had exhausted themselves trying various unsuccessful escape routes. Their map was sodden tissue paper and their tiny compass looked like it had come out of a Christmas cracker.

We fumbled our way to Mickledore on a bearing then descended to Wasdale where they were camped. A hot shower convinced me that I was much better off there than at my original destination, a wild camp at Sprinkling Tarn.

Things improved further when, in their gratitude, my new-found friends treated me to an evening of spag bol and Dutch lager.

Ishmael Burdeau
Brighton

Having climbed Ben Nevis and Snowdon in summer 2002 with my seven-year-old son Milo, we both felt the year wouldn't be complete without an attempt on the 'easiest' of the Three Peaks – Scafell Pike.

When the day of our climb dawned, the rain was falling steadily, a thick mist enveloped the surrounding fells, and the weather forecast spoke only vaguely of the possibility of things clearing up in the afternoon. Not exactly ideal conditions for covering the 10+ miles between Honister and Wasdale!

We managed to get lost in thick fog near the top of Green Gable. At this point I was thinking of leaving Scafell Pike for next year, but Milo wouldn't hear of it. After retracing our steps (and climbing Green Gable not once but twice), we finally managed to catch a glimpse of our prize through the mist.

Near Sprinkling Tarn the rain suddenly cleared, revealing the wild beauty of our surroundings. Milo's strength was beginning to wane, but after a few squares of chocolate and with our goal within sight, his energy returned.

Standing on the summit, we could see beautiful lakes and mountains in every direction for miles around. Our sense of achievement came as much from the journey of eight hours we had taken to get to this spot as it did from merely standing on the highest point in England.

As we made our weary but rapid decent to Wasdale on that postcard-perfect evening, with the still waters of the lake reflecting a red sunset, Milo announced his retirement from mountaineering. Once you've done the Three Peaks, he reasoned, there is nothing left worth climbing! After a rest, however, he soon changed his mind when I told him of some of the other challenges out there.

LOCATION	**LAKE DISTRICT**
HEIGHT	**736m (2,403ft)**
SUMMIT GR	**NY282074**

Harrison Stickle

Imagine the scene: you're in the final of *University Challenge*. It's a dead heat between Brownnose College, Toffsford, and your team, the University of Outdoors Life. The studio lights are beating down on you. One minute to go. Jeremy Paxperson arches his terrible brow and says, "The decider, then. Your final starter for ten: where is the oldest factory in Britain?" Would you jam your finger down on the buzzer to snatch the crown from the defending champions? Or would you um and er with the Toffsford team? In fact the answer is the Langdale Pikes – but not a lot of people know that.

To be sure of winning *Universally Challenged*, you need to know about the Kendal hill-walker who, just after the war, found what looked like a stone axehead in a gully on Pike o'Stickle. Before you could say 'porcellinite band', archaeologists had discovered that the slopes of the Pikes were littered with faulty axeheads: the rejects from Britain's oldest factory. About 5,500 years ago this was the only place a forward-thinking Neolithic would even consider buying his axe ("Honestly, Ug darling, if you want quality you've simply got to have a Langdale"). Heads from the Langdale factory were chipped out of a band of porcellinite only 10m thick. This very fine sandstone was then sent down to the coast to be honed

Harrison Stickle – your
starter for ten.
JEREMY ASHCROFT

Words **Piers Pickard**

FOLLOW IN THE FOOTSTEPS OF NEOLITHIC MAN TO THE SITE OF BRITAIN'S FIRST FACTORY!

and polished with coarser local sandstone. Langdale axes were exported all over Britain, and have even been found in Ireland, the Low Countries and Germany, proving that trade and communications in Neolithic times were... well, not so Neolithic.

The Pikes have everything. The loftiest of the five, Harrison Stickle, isn't a giant by anybody's standards – it tops out at a respectable, if not earth-shattering, 736m. But in terms of variety and breadth of appeal, the Pikes roundly beat every

other mountain in Britain. Almost every visitor to the Lake District, no matter how little interest they normally take in mountains, will take a drive up Langdale and marvel at the steep rockiness of Harrison Stickle towering above them. Step into any Lakeland hotel or craft shop, and the walls will be festooned with amateurish blue and purple watercolours with the words 'The Langdale Pikes viewed from Langdale' scribbled in pencil in the corner.

So what's their secret? Approached from the north,

Harrison Stickle looks like a minor dimple on a gently rising moor. Of the other four Pikes – Pavey Ark, Thorn Crag, Loft Crag and Pike o'Stickle – only the latter shows any sort of profile against the skyline.

But from Langdale, it's a different story. Their southern slopes surge over 2,000 vertical feet in just half a mile to the cairn on Harrison Stickle. Their steep-sided profile dominates a glimpse into central Lakeland as you head north on the M6. Gimmer Crag stands proud against the skyline and is known as the best climbing crag in the valley; it's also one of the finest in England. For scramblers, there is no area richer in classics: Jack's Rake with its lightning-bolt slash across vertical Pavey Ark; the faces of both Harrison Stickle and Pike o'Stickle; and Dungeon Ghyll, a sodden classic described long ago by Wordsworth in his poem *The Idle Shepherd Boys*.

But the slopes of Harrison Stickle have been popular for a lot longer than Wordsworth could have guessed. Even so, the Pikes probably didn't see the amount of traffic they see today – the path up Stickle Ghyll to the tarn is trodden by half a million feet every year, making it one of the busiest in the Lakes. At the top of it, you can cross the ghyll where it flows from the tarn over a dam. This was built in the 19th century to safeguard a water supply for the main Langdale factory of the industrial era – the gunpowder works at Elterwater. The explosives they made there were essential for extracting a different rock from the hillsides: Lakeland slate.

But if the Langdale Pikes, with their fine walking, scrambling and climbing, their views and their archaeology, are to stake their claim as the UK mountain that truly has everything, they need a legendary watering-hole. And this they have in the shape of the Old Dungeon Ghyll Hotel. All the famous names of British mountaineering have passed through the doors of the Climbers' Bar. In the Forties and Fifties, it was used for climbing club dinners by most of John Hunt's Everest team. In later years, it was where Chris Bonington went after his first British ascent of the north face of the Eiger. He practised his slideshow lecture on the drinkers in the bar before giving the real thing in Keswick.

So when you stand on Harrison Stickle's summit, enjoy the view knowing that you have everything you need around you on Britain's most complete mountain.

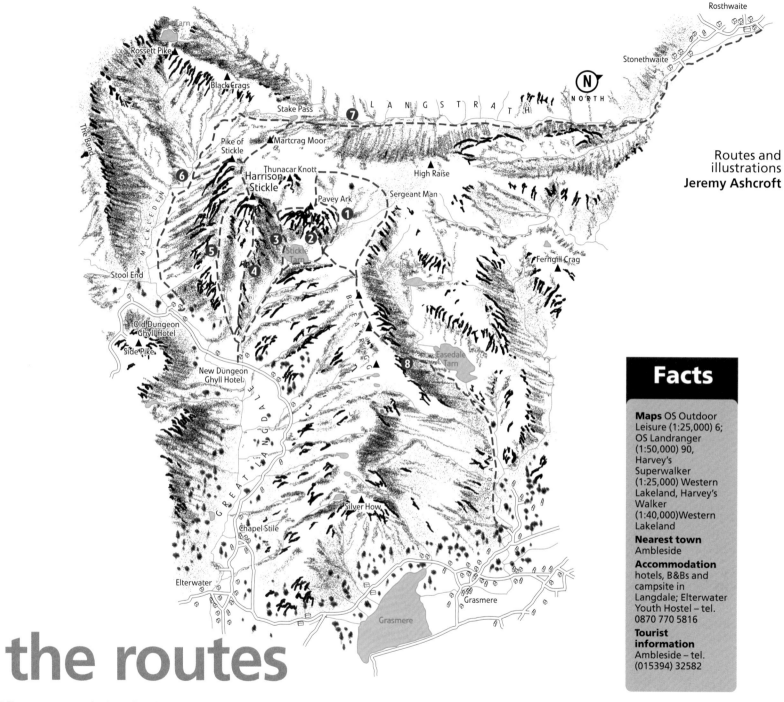

Rosthwaite

Stonethwaite

L A N G S T R A T H

Stake Pass

Tarn

Rossett Pike ▲

Black Crags ▲

The Band

Pike of Stickle ▲

▲ Martcrag Moor

Thunacar Knott ▲

Harrison Stickle

Pavey Ark

M I C K L E D E N

Stool End

Sergeant Man

High Raise ▲

Ferngill Crag ▲

Stickle Tarn

B L E A R I G G

Col Gill

Easedale Tarn

Old Dungeon Ghyll Hotel

Side Pike ▲

New Dungeon Ghyll Hotel

G R E A T   L A N G D A L E

E A S E D A L E

Silver How ▲

Chapel Stile

Elterwater

Grasmere

Grasmere

N NORTH

Routes and illustrations
Jeremy Ashcroft

Facts

Maps OS Outdoor Leisure (1:25,000) 6; OS Landranger (1:50,000) 90, Harvey's Superwalker (1:25,000) Western Lakeland, Harvey's Walker (1:40,000)Western Lakeland

Nearest town Ambleside

Accommodation hotels, B&Bs and campsite in Langdale; Elterwater Youth Hostel – tel. 0870 770 5816

Tourist information Ambleside – tel. (015394) 32582

the routes

● The times given are for the walk to the summit only – not there and back.

1 NORTH RAKE OF PAVEY ARK

An easy grassy rake that climbs to the top of Pavey Ark but misses out all the tricky rock bits.
Start New Dungeon Ghyll Hotel (NY295065)

Distance 3km (2 miles)
Time 1½-2 hours
Height gain 687m
Terrain steep-sided ghyll, rocky corrie with tarn, grassy rake and rocky summits
Difficulty intermediate
Popularity busy

Route Climb NW up the Mill Gill path to Stickle Tarn then skirt N around the tarn to gain the foot of the grassy rake on the eastern extremity of Pavey Ark. This is North Rake; climb it W to the summit of Pavey Ark then descend W from the summit to cross a broad col to the summit of Harrison Stickle.

2 JACK'S RAKE

Gains the top of Pavey Ark by the classic scramble of Jack's Rake. Relatively easy but you will need a good head for heights as the top section is particularly exposed.

Start New Dungeon Ghyll Hotel **(NY295065)**
Distance 3km (2 miles)
Time 1½-2 hours
Height gain 687m
Terrain steep-sided ghyll, rocky corrie with tarn, steep rocky rake and rocky summits
Difficulty intermediate (Grade 1 scramble, Grade 1 winter climb)
Popularity busy

Route Climb NW up the Mill Gill path to Stickle Tarn then skirt N around the tarn to gain the foot of Pavey Ark. Jack's Rake follows a rising traverse across the crags of Pavey Ark. It ends 100m SW of Pavey Ark's summit. From the summit descend W and cross the broad col to the summit of Harrison Stickle.

3 EASTERN COMBE FROM STICKLE TARN

A well-trodden and easy route up the high combe on the eastern side of Harrison Stickle's summit cone. A safe route off in bad weather.

Start New Dungeon Ghyll Hotel **(NY295065)**
Distance 2.5km (1½ miles)
Time 1½ hours
Height gain 644m
Terrain steep-sided ghyll, rocky corrie with tarn, steep corrie, broad col and rocky summit
Difficulty easy
Popularity busy

Route Climb NW up the Mill Gill path to Stickle Tarn then skirt W around the tarn. From its western corner climb W up the steep combe to the broad col between Pavey Ark and Harrison Stickle. Turn L and climb SW to the summit of Harrison Stickle.

4 PIKE HOW ROUTE

A superb, airy route up the knobbly south-eastern ridge. The views are outstanding and the ground crossed, although not technically too difficult, is always exciting.

Start New Dungeon Ghyll Hotel **(NY295065)**
Distance 2km (1¼ miles)
Time 1½ hours
Height gain 654m
Terrain steep fellside, rocky knoll, steep-sided ghyll, crags and rocky summit cone
Difficulty intermediate
Popularity moderate

Route Follow the Dungeon Ghyll path to the fork. Take the R branch and follow it NW on to Pike How. Rejoin the path and follow it as it climbs NW to the head of Dungeon Ghyll. At the path junction turn NE and follow it to the summit of Harrison Stickle.

5 THORN CRAG PATH

A devious route that zigzags through some steep and rocky ground. Easy to follow with superb views.

Start New Dungeon Ghyll Hotel **(NY295065)**
Distance 2km (1¼ miles)
Time 1½ hours
Height gain 644m
Terrain steep fellside, broad ridge, grassy plateau and rocky summit cone
Difficulty intermediate
Popularity busy

Route Follow the Dungeon Ghyll path to the fork. Follow L branch W then NW up the broad ridge and around the SW-facing flank of Thorn Crag. On the plateau, turn NE to cross the head of Dungeon Ghyll and reach the summit of Harrison Stickle.

6 STAKE PASS

Uses the old 'packhorse' route that climbs in a series of neat zigzags from the depths of Mickleden then sneaks in round the back across the high-level plateau of Martcrag Moor

Start Old Dungeon Ghyll Hotel **(NY284061)**
Distance 7km (4½ miles)
Time 2½ hours
Height gain 660m
Terrain long steep-sided valley, steep zigzags, high moorland, grassy plateau and rocky summit
Difficulty intermediate
Popularity moderate

Route Follow the good track W then NW along Mickleden to the foot of Stake Pass. Climb the zigzags N to the top of Stake Pass then turn R and follow the path SE over Martcrag Moor, past Pike of Stickle then E past the top of Dungeon Ghyll to the summit cone of Harrison Stickle.

7 LANGSTRATH

A long approach from Borrowdale via the deep and interesting valley of Langstrath.

Start Rosthwaite **(NY258148)**
Distance 9.5km (6 miles)
Time 3-4 hours
Height gain 636m
Terrain long remote valley, steep zigzags, high moorland, grassy plateau and rocky summit
Difficulty intermediate
Popularity quiet

Route From Rosthwaite cross Stonethwaite Beck by the road. Turn immediately R, join the bridleway and follow it SE to the Greenup Beck junction then SW up Langstrath to the foot of Stake Pass. Climb the zigzags S to the top of Stake Pass then turn L and follow the path SE over Martcrag Moor, past Pike of Stickle then E past the top of Dungeon Ghyll to the summit cone of Harrison Stickle.

8 EASEDALE AND SERGEANT MAN

A long but logical route from Grasmere that gains Sergeant Man on the eastern edge of the Langdale Pikes plateau in a series of steps. First up to Easedale Tarn, secondly on to Blea Rigg then finally on to Pavey Ark.

Start Grasmere **(NY335074)**
Distance 8km (5 miles)
Time 2½-3 hours
Height gain 667m
Terrain open valley, stepped hanging corries with tarns, high-level ridge, grassy plateau and rocky summit cone
Difficulty intermediate
Popularity quiet

Route From Grasmere follow the Easedale Road then bridleway W to Easedale Tarn. Continue W past tarn on narrow path and up past Belles Knott to rough scree-filled combe. Climb through combe to gain the NW end of Blea Rigg. Walk NW on a faint path to Sergeant Man then head W and then S to Thunacar Knott. More faint paths lead SE to Pavey Ark. From the summit descend W and cross the broad col to the summit of Harrison Stickle.

"I've climbed it"

Rita Heap Keighley

Seeing Harrison Stickle mentioned in Trail brought happy memories flooding back. I was in the sixth form at Southport High School for Girls. One teacher wanted to introduce us to the hills and mountains, and so she took a small group of us to the Lake District for a few days. Some of us had only seen pictures of mountains, as travel was very restricted during the war and the Southport area is very flat!

We went on public transport and stayed at Elterwater Youth Hostel. We spent our days walking up hills and down dales, and thoroughly enjoyed ourselves. We had no special equipment or clothing as rationing was still in force and, as far as I can remember, we wore our school uniform, gabardine coats and outdoor shoes, with a pair of plimsolls for emergencies! Girls did not usually wear trousers in those days. None of us thought of carrying even a bottle of water (vital equipment today!).

As you might imagine, scaling the heights of Harrison Stickle was the high spot of the trip for me, especially as the weather was clear and the views spectacular.

I have kept my love of walking and regularly visit the Lake District and the Yorkshire Dales. I climbed my first Munro at 70, so my love of mountains has never faded.

Thank you and Harrison Stickle for reviving such happy memories of my past. Sadly I don't have a photo from my school trip, so I have enclosed one of me on Cat Bells last autumn.

John & Alison Whalley Newcastle upon Tyne

For our 15th wedding anniversary we decided that we had earned a break from the children, and we booked into Codale Tarn for the night. We woke at 6am to a scorching day and a brilliant view of Easedale and a distant Grasmere, broken only by a few wispy strands of mist. After a quick wash in the cold bath, a short walk-scramble up the nearby grassy ledge led to the walk towards Sergeant Man, then Thunacar Knott, and finally the wide plateau to the Langdale Pikes.

The route was fairly busy with individual walkers, families and one larger party scrambling up the side of Pavey Ark – all heading towards the Harrison Stickle magnet. A swift haul over the rocky magnet, and we were there...

From the summit, we looked one way to the neighbouring Pike of Stickle, a bit like a beehive hairdo, and the other way along the stretch of the Langdale Valley and the mini-cars running along the track to Grasmere. Somewhere down there was a pint of Old Peculier at the Old Dungeon Ghyll. The walk back down to Great Langdale via the Stake Pass and Mickleden felt as long as 15 years of marriage (but not really!).

LOCATION	**LAKE DISTRICT**
HEIGHT	**852m (2,791ft)**
SUMMIT GR	**NY175204**

Grasmoor

Beloved of bards and botanists, this 'violet' hill has a violent past.

Words Piers Pickard

"A most sublime crag, of a violet colour, patched here and there with islands of heath plant, and wrinkled and guttered most picturesquely." Samuel Taylor Coleridge may have been an opium addict, but he knew a good mountain from a field full of poppies. He and William Wordsworth enjoyed a peaceful walk over Grasmoor during their famous tour of the Lake District in 1799.

Had they been there 694 years earlier though, their impressions would have been very different, as this giant of the north-western fells is steeped in violent Norse history.

The Norman invasion of 1066 took 26 years to rumble up to Cumbria, when William II ousted the Anglo-Saxon King Dolfin. But the mainly Norse locals weren't too happy about southerners swanning around the Lakes as though they owned the place. In 1105 the Viking Earl Boethar lured William Meschin's Norman army into the valley of Rannerdale on the south side of Grasmoor, then sprang his well-planned ambush. It was a victory almost as good as the more recent one between the Danes and the French at the World Cup. Seven centuries later, perhaps Coleridge and Wordsworth saw the bluebells of Rannerdale on their walk. They supposedly mark the spots where the Frenchies fell.

In fact, Grasmoor is the floweriest mountain in the Lakes, so it was an ideal place for these two Romantic poets to wander lonely as the lyrical luvvies that they were. More flora grows here than on any other hill, but it is the berries that rule the rooting roost. Bilberry, cowberry and crowberry dominate, with the bilberries reaching a whopping size in July and August. This is because the steep screes around the mountain are too slippy for the sheep to find purchase on, so they can't get close enough for a nibble. But look as you might, you won't find the Lakes' rarest plant among the wild flowers here. To see the red alpine catchfly, you need to stroll north-east for a mile over the broad summit meadow to Hobcarton Crag.

On your way you will follow the course of Gasgale Gill, which borders the north side of Grasmoor. Gasgale too is old Norse, meaning 'a ravine where there are goat herders' huts', giving us a clue as to what the Vikings did here when

Keswick • Mide
• Kendal
Skipton •

Grasmoor looms large beyond Loweswater's lily pads.

ASHLEY COOPER

they weren't massacring the Normans. It could certainly explain the role of the ancient homestead at the bottom of the ghyll (NY159210).

There is another goat link on the west side of the mountain, where Grasmoor is at its most impressive. It looms over the blue-grey of Crummock Water, soaring nearly half a mile into the sky as a towering pyramid of rock and scree. No other mountain in the Lakes looks as impressive from the roadside. Beyond grassy verges the ground gradually steepens, eventually rising to a near-vertical wall of broken rock, lightning-split by two sinister gullies. One of these is Lorton Gully, a three-star, Grade 3S scramble that is worthy of the face it cleaves. Lorton is another Norse word, meaning 'Hlora's farmstead'. Hlora was the stepmum of the god Thor, who rode a mighty cart across the heavens pulled by the fearsome goats (fearsome goats?!) Tanngniostir (Toothcracker) and Tanngrisnir (Toothgnasher). Sparks flew from their hooves and teeth, and the iron-rimmed wheels of the cart rumbled like thunder.

Grasmoor isn't a mountain that tops most people's favourites list, but with its history, its rich flora, and its massive west face, it is easy to understand why the great Lakeland writer Harry Griffin wrote in *The Roof of England*: "Some people may agree that Grasmoor, with its acres of smoothly sloping turf, can be a dull mountain in places but, using your imagination quite a lot and choosing the right day, you could compare its great wall of broken crags towering over Crummock Water with the way the North Wall of the Eiger dominates Lauterbrunnen and the Grindelwald valley." So there!

the routes

● The times given are for the walk to the summit only – not there and back.

1 WHITELESS PIKE ROUTE

Whiteless Pike abuts the south side of the Grasmoor/Crag Hill massif. Its connecting ridge, Whiteless Edge, provides a pleasant, airy approach from the Buttermere side with stunning views south towards High Stile, Great Gable and Pillar.

Start Buttermere **(NY174172)**
Distance 4.6km (2¾ miles)
Time 2½ hours
Height gain 721m
Terrain steep fellside, high rounded ridges and summit plateau
Difficulty easy
Popularity moderate

Route You gain Whiteless Pike by taking the steep path NE from Buttermere onto Whiteless Breast then N onto Whiteless Pike. You then follow the crest of Whiteless Edge direct to the col below Crag Hill from where an easy ascent W leads to Grasmoor's summit.

2 LAD HOWS ROUTE

Lad Hows is a truncated spur on the south side of Grasmoor which provides a steady stepped route to the summit plateau from the side of Crummock Water.

Start Cinderdale Beck car park **(NY163193)**
Distance 3.5km (2¼ miles)
Time 2 hours
Height gain 746m
Terrain steep fellside, high rounded ridges and summit plateau
Difficulty easy
Popularity moderate

ASHLEY COOPER

Route From the car park take the path that zigzags generally ENE to the small summit of Lad Hows. Continue NE along the rounded ridge then turn N as it steepens into the south flanks of Grasmoor. As you reach the plateau trend W to the summit cairn.

3 RED GILL

A steep, unremitting slog NE up the shallow hanging corrie formed by Red Gill. A technically easier alternative to the routes on Grasmoor End or for people who enjoy steep unremitting slogs!

Start Crummock Water car park **(NY162195)**
Distance 1.8km (1 mile)
Time 1½-2 hours
Height gain 746m
Terrain steep fellside, scree, steep head wall and grassy summit plateau
Difficulty intermediate
Popularity quiet

Route From the car park climb steeply E then NE up Red Gill to gain the western shoulder of Grasmoor. On the easier ground of the rounded summit ridge head E to the summit cairn and shelter.

4 LORTON GULLY

Entertaining from start to finish, Lorton Gully is a classic gully scramble. You follow the bed from the scree fan at the base of Grasmoor End. This should only be undertaken in dry conditions – the presence of water makes it considerably

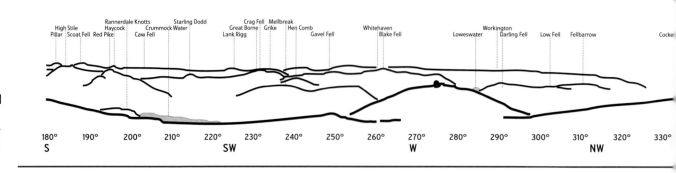

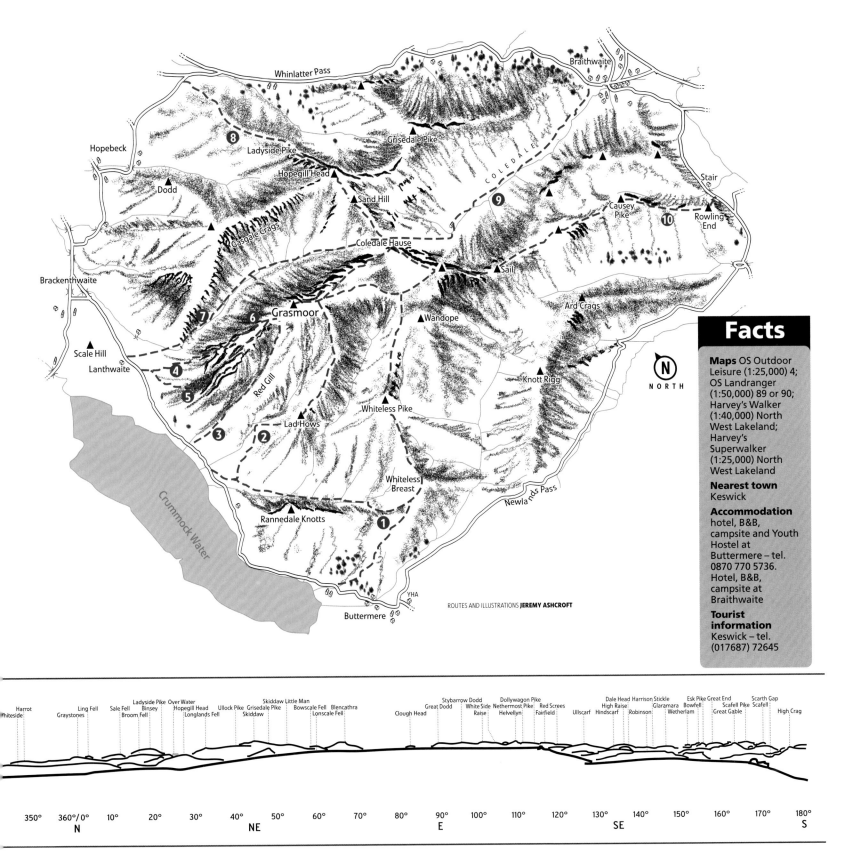

Whinlatter Pass

Braithwaite

COLEDALE

Hopebeck

⑧ Ladyside Pike

Grisedale Pike

Stair

Dodd

Hopegill Head

Sand Hill

⑨

Causey Pike

⑩ Rowling End

Gasgale Crags

Coledale Hause

Sail

Brackenthwaite

⑦ ⑥ Grasmoor

Wandope

Ard Crags

Scale Hill

Lanthwaite

④

Red Gill

⑤

Knott Rigg

③ ② Lad Hows

Whiteless Pike

Crummock Water

Whiteless Breast

Newlands Pass

Rannedale Knotts

① ⑩

YHA

ROUTES AND ILLUSTRATIONS **JEREMY ASHCROFT**

Buttermere

N NORTH

Facts

Maps OS Outdoor Leisure (1:25,000) 4; OS Landranger (1:50,000) 89 or 90; Harvey's Walker (1:40,000) North West Lakeland; Harvey's Superwalker (1:25,000) North West Lakeland

Nearest town Keswick

Accommodation hotel, B&B, campsite and Youth Hostel at Buttermere – tel. 0870 770 5736. Hotel, B&B, campsite at Braithwaite

Tourist information Keswick – tel. (017687) 72645

Harrot
Whiteside
Ling Fell
Graystones
Sale Fell
Broom Fell
Ladyside Pike
Binsey
Over Water
Hopegill Head
Longlands Fell
Ullock Pike
Skiddaw Little Man
Grisedale Pike
Skiddaw
Bowscale Fell
Lonscale Fell
Blencathra
Clough Head
Stybarrow Dodd
Great Dodd
White Side
Raise
Dollywagon Pike
Nethermost Pike
Helvellyn
Red Screes
Fairfield
Ullscarf
Dale Head
High Raise
Hindscarf
Harrison Stickle
Glaramara
Robinson
Wetherlam
Esk Pike
Bowfell
Great End
Scafell Pike
Scafell
Great Gable
Scarth Gap
High Crag

350° 360°/0° 10° 20° 30° 40° 50° 60° 70° 80° 90° 100° 110° 120° 130° 140° 150° 160° 170° 180°
N   NE   E   SE   S

harder. The crux of the scramble is at mid-height and consists of a chockstone which requires fairly acrobatic bridging moves to pass, and a steep stepped wall. Climbing the crux section will usually require the use of a rope.

Start Lanthwaite car park **(NY158206)**
Distance 1.8km (1 mile)
Time 3-4 hours
Height gain 746m
Terrain long gully among steep, broken crags and grassy summit plateau
Difficulty Grade 3 scramble (top end of the grade!)
Popularity quiet

Route Climb the open fellside SE to the base of Grasmoor End. Lorton Gully is the distinctive Y-shaped gully just a touch left of centre of the crag (the most visible line on the crag). Enter the gully and climb its bed to the first steepening; if you have problems here retreat, as the crux section is harder still. At the first part of the crux, the chockstone, the best ploy is to bridge past it until it is possible to clamber onto its top. At the back of the bay above the chockstone is the second part of the crux: a steep exposed wall; climb this from left to right. You escape another bay above the wall by making a traverse left to right, on the right wall, to gain easier ground. Traverse back into the bed of the gully above the bay and continue to climb this. A number of steps provide interest until the gully splits below a steep head wall. Take the vague left branch and follow its general line out onto the NW ridge which you follow onto the summit plateau.

5 GRASMOOR END ARÊTE

The northern edge of the crags of Grasmoor end forms a rocky arête which provides an exciting yet easy scramble.

Start Lanthwaite car park **(NY158206)**
Distance 1.8km (1 mile)
Time 2 hours
Height gain 746m
Terrain steep fellside, scree, broken crags, rocky arête and grassy summit plateau
Difficulty strenuous (involves some easy scrambling)
Popularity quiet

Route The arête starts at a distinct pinnacle which you reach from the footbridge across Liza Beck. Climb SE straight up the fellside then, at the crags, zigzag up the terraces and rakes onto a subsidiary arête which climbs onto the pinnacle. Follow the main arête as it climbs high above Grasmoor End onto the summit plateau.

6 DOVE CRAGS RIDGE

A steep but interesting route that climbs the grassy arête on the western edge of Dove Crags.

Start Lanthwaite car park **(NY158206)**
Distance 2.6km (1½ miles)
Time 2 hours
Height gain 746m
Terrain steep-sided valley, steep fellside, steep grassy ridge and grassy summit plateau
Difficulty intermediate
Popularity quiet

Route You reach the base of the arête from the path up Gasgale Gill. The initial climb is up steep grass and heather but it soon becomes more interesting as you gain height and dramatic views into the depths of Dove Crags open out. As the arête merges with the summit plateau, swing W to head for the summit cairn.

7 GASGALE GILL

Gains the eastern end of Grasmoor's summit plateau via an easy ascent along the bottom of Gasgale Gill then over pleasant grass from Coledale Hause. The best descent route in poor conditions.

Start Lanthwaite car park **NY158206**
Distance 5.8km (3½ miles)
Time 2-2½ hours
Height gain 746m
Terrain steep-sided valley, broad col, stony ghyll, grassy fellside and grassy summit plateau
Difficulty easy
Popularity moderate

Route Gains height steadily along the course of Gasgale Gill to Coledale Hause then swings S to gain the col on the W side of Crag Hill. From here a steady climb W leads onto the summit plateau and then to Grasmoor's summit cairn.

8 NORTH RIDGE OF HOPEGILL HEAD

An excellent route from Lorton Vale taking in a simple scramble up the fine north ridge of Hopegill.

Start minor road near Hopebeck **(NY175253)**
Distance 6.8 km (4¼ miles)
Time 2½-3 hours
Height gain 759m
Terrain steep fellside, rounded ridge, rocky arête, rocky summit, broad col, stony ghyll, grassy fellside and grassy summit plateau
Difficulty strenuous (the final arête on Hopegill Head involves easy scrambling bordering on Grade 1)
Popularity quiet

Route From the minor road climb S onto the rounded NW ridge of Ladyside Pike. Climb its crest over Ladyside Pike and on towards Hopegill Head. As the ridge gains height it steepens and narrows considerably, providing a superb finish right to the summit rocks of Hopegill Head. Descend S to Coledale Hause then gain the col on the W side of Crag Hill. From here a steady climb W leads onto the summit plateau and then to Grasmoor's summit cairn.

9 COLEDALE ROUTE

A long steady approach along the depths of Coledale providing the most direct approach from the Braithwaite/Keswick side.

ASHLEY COOPER

Start Braithwaite (**NY227237**)
Distance 6.5km (4 miles)
Time 2½ hours
Height gain 751m
Terrain steep-sided valley, broad col, stony col, grassy fellside and grassy summit plateau
Difficulty easy
Popularity moderate

Route Follow the good track along Coledale and cross the beck downstream of the mine buildings. Follow the deteriorating track to Coledale Hause then gain the col on the W side of Crag Hill. From here a steady climb W leads onto the summit plateau and then to Grasmoor's summit cairn.

10 CAUSEY PIKE ROUTE

A long ridge approach that takes in the fine summits of Causey Pike and Crag Hill with an easy scramble thrown in for good measure.

Start Stair (**NY233212**)
Distance 6.5km (4 miles)
Time 3-3½ hours
Height gain 835m
Terrain steep fellside, long mountain ridge, steep rocky ridge, stony summit, grassy fellside and grassy summit plateau
Difficulty intermediate
Popularity moderate

Route From the bridge over Stonycroft Gill take the path SSW onto Rowling End. From here turn W and follow the steadily climbing ridge over Causey Pike and Sail to make the final steep ascent to Crag Hill. Continue W from Crag Hill and descend to the col. From here a steady climb W leads onto the summit plateau and then to Grasmoor's summit.

"I've climbed it"

Chris Thomas Hazelrigg

One day when we were both off together (and had a babysitter), the wife and I took a trip to Grasmoor. Parking at Lanthwaite, we saw Grasmoor's summit and the ridge around to it were draped in thick fog. On reaching the top of Whiteside we were assaulted by the winds screaming in from the Irish Sea. However, the fog failed to clear sufficiently for us to see our route.

Descending to Coledale Hause, I had to hold onto the wife to stop her blowing away. The valley between Crag Hill and Grasmoor still had a deep covering of snow; then came the final push to the summit. Visibility was now down to a hand in front of the face. So it was out with the trusty compass, the missus walking in front at the limit of visibility and me giving her directions and reassurance: we were not lost, just topographically relocated.

Lunching at Grasmoor's summit shelter, the fog lifted to give us magnificent views towards the Solway Firth and Scotland. Then the weather closed its curtains on us. We set off for the path descending by Lad Hows towards Crummock Water. But it proved totally elusive, so we backtracked our route to Coledale Hause and descended via the track that runs down parallel with Liza Beck between Whiteside and Grasmoor.

This thoroughly enjoyable route was one of the easiest descents that I can remember; and the views, although limited, were still spectacular.

What we'd thought would be a quick stroll turned out to be both challenging and rewarding. I only hope it's not too long before similar rewards can be experienced again.

PS. Anyone fancy a bit of babysitting?

Chris Howe Kingsthorpe

I woke up one August morning to crystal-clear skies, so I ran to see if my neighbour was free for a trip to Crummock Water. I was in luck. We started on Whiteside and went over the tops of Gasgale Crags (giving great views of Grasmoor) before reaching the summit of Hopegill Head. Avoiding two guys on mobiles reserving

tables for dinner, we trotted over Sand Hill and into Coledale Hause, up the little valley below Eel Crag, and eventually turned west and headed for the summit.

Reaching the summit cairn was the pinnacle of fell-walking for me. The view over to a blue Crummock Water was breathtaking, but it was the scene to the south that stole the day. That view to the Scafell massif is tattooed on my memory, and for me is the Lakes' best.

LOCATION	SOUTHERN HIGHLANDS
HEIGHT	1214m (3,982ft)
SUMMIT GR	636414

Ben Lawers

This is a whole lot of mountain – even if a group back in 1878 felt it needed a bit of cosmetic enhancement...

Worried about your height? Then there's no better way to draw attention to the fact than by marching around in a pair of snakeskin Cuban heels or the kind of psychedelic platform boots favoured by poodle-permed, prog rock bands. They might give you the lift you so badly long for, but no-one's impressed by the sight of you teetering around on six inches of shoe leather. The same thing goes for mountains.

Facts

Maps OS Landranger (1:50,000) 51, Harveys Superwalker (1:25,000) & Harveys Walker (1:40,000) Ben Lawers

Nearest town Killin

Accommodation Youth Hostel – tel. (01567) 820546, B&Bs and hotels in

As so often happens with inanimate objects, Ben Lawers wasn't consulted when an altitude-enhancing edifice was erected at its summit some 123 years ago. Thirty men and two stone masons, led by the Glaswegian Malcolm Ferguson, took it upon themselves to construct the seven-metre-high tower they hoped would elevate the Munro into the elite ranks of Scottish 4,000ft peaks. While no-one was fooled by this bit of statistical jiggery-pokery, it had the potential to leave Ben Lawers with a long-term altitude complex; one that, as it turned out, would last a lot longer than the tower itself.

Today only a stump of that building remains, clearly marking the summit. But while the mountain has officially sunk back to 1214m (that's 3,981.9ft to you, granddad), its reputation among mountain enthusiasts has had something of a growth spurt.

One of seven Munros in the Ben Lawers group, it stands head, if not shoulders, above its neighbours. In fact, it's a clear 96m higher than local bad boys Meall Garbh and An Stuc. This ridge of peaks measures a cool 12km long and never drops below 780m, which makes it the biggest single massif in the Southern Highlands. It's unsurpassed in this area in terms of height and grandeur, and Ben Lawers is the jewel in its alpine crown.

Located to the north-west of Loch Tay in the Southern Highlands, there's some superb walking to be had here. A reasonably fit hill-walker (especially one with a willing car driver to ferry them around) should be able to knock off all seven peaks in a day. But if you really want to make the most of your time here, you're advised to take a full three days to sample its delights.

Of course, it's Ben Lawers that is the real boot magnet. As Britain's tenth highest mountain and one of the most popular Munros, it offers a host of accessible routes. It's craggy in places, but its broad, smooth ridges make this a viable climb, even in winter.

When the snow does come, you can expect to find the place crawling with ski-mountaineers. Back in the 1930s, Ben Lawers was the focal point of skiing in Scotland. In the 1950s there was even a rudimentary tow rope to pull skiers to the top. You won't find many downhillers these days, but ski-mountaineers still 'slip-slide' across its wintry slopes.

Come spring, a different breed begins scouring the sides of the mountain: amateur botanists. This area is famed for its wild alpine plants, including several species of saxifrage, rare ferns and mosses, which take refuge in the least accessible parts of the mountain. It's the rich alkaline soil here that makes it such a fertile area for these plants. In fact, it's so important that The National Trust for Scotland bought the southern side of Ben Lawers in 1950.

Of course, popularity has its price and mountains generally pay in the globally accepted currency of path erosion and environmental degradation. The track from the National Trust hut is the one most often used by walkers, and it has required major repair work of late. So fragile is the ecosystem here that areas beneath the mountain have also been closed for regeneration. On a purely selfish note though, it's not too difficult to avoid the crowds: simply use the route suggestions that follow to keep out of their way.

And when you next plant your feet on its 3,981.9ft summit, don't worry too much about the 18.1ft that could have lifted Ben Lawers into the big league. Size isn't important; it's how you climb it that counts.

The Ben Lawers range from the roadhead at Glen Ogle.

PAUL MILLIGAN

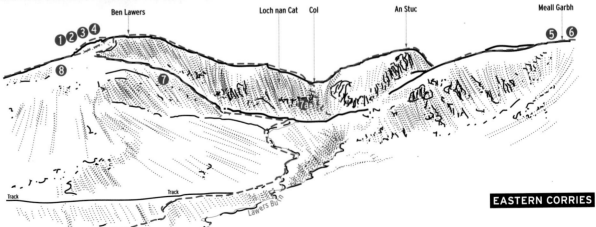

EASTERN CORRIES

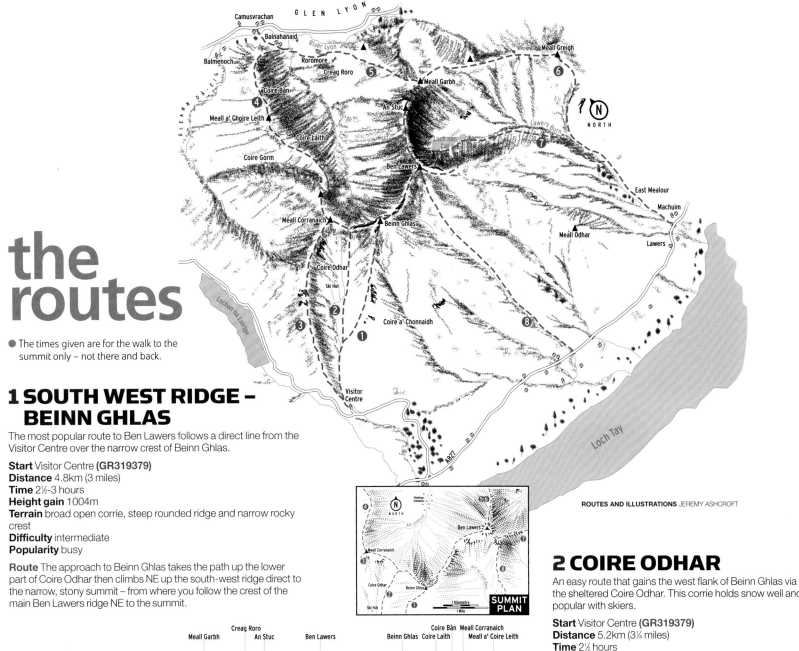

the routes

● The times given are for the walk to the summit only – not there and back.

ROUTES AND ILLUSTRATIONS JEREMY ASHCROFT

1 SOUTH WEST RIDGE – BEINN GHLAS

The most popular route to Ben Lawers follows a direct line from the Visitor Centre over the narrow crest of Beinn Ghlas.

Start Visitor Centre **(GR319379)**
Distance 4.8km (3 miles)
Time 2½-3 hours
Height gain 1004m
Terrain broad open corrie, steep rounded ridge and narrow rocky crest
Difficulty intermediate
Popularity busy

Route The approach to Beinn Ghlas takes the path up the lower part of Coire Odhar then climbs NE up the south-west ridge direct to the narrow, stony summit – from where you follow the crest of the main Ben Lawers ridge NE to the summit.

2 COIRE ODHAR

An easy route that gains the west flank of Beinn Ghlas via the sheltered Coire Odhar. This corrie holds snow well and is popular with skiers.

Start Visitor Centre **(GR319379)**
Distance 5.2km (3¼ miles)
Time 2½ hours
Height gain 789m
Terrain broad open corrie, steep-sided corrie, broad col, rocky corrie and steep ridge
Difficulty intermediate
Popularity moderate

Route From the Visitor Centre follow the main path N up through Coire Odhar. Gain the col at its head to join a devious path that skirts the N side of Beinn Ghlas to the col on the SW side of Ben Lawers' summit pyramid, from where you can follow the main ridge path to the summit.

3 SOUTH RIDGE – MEALL CORRANAICH

Meall Corranaich can easily be included in an ascent of Ben Lawers from the Visitor Centre by climbing the long, enclosing ridge on the west side of Coire Odhar.

Start Visitor Centre **(GR319379)**
Distance 6.4km (4 miles)
Time 3-3½ hours **Height gain** 1090m
Terrain broad open corrie, high ridges, broad col and narrow main ridge
Difficulty strenuous
Popularity quiet

Route The steady ascent N up the south ridge of Meall Corranaich curves around the head of Coire Odhar to the summit pyramid and affords fine views of Beinn Ghlas and Lochan na Lair. From the summit of Meall Corranaich, turn SE and descend the steep ridge to the broad col at the head of Coire Odhar. From the col, steep slopes lead SE to Beinn Ghlas – from where you follow the crest of the main ridge NE to the summit.

4 MEALL A' CHOIRE LÉITH ROUTE

The western slopes of Ben Lawers fall away steeply into the deep glen occupied by the Allt a' Chobhair; the opposite side of this glen is a long switchback ridge made up by two fine mountains: Meall a' Choire Leith and Meall Corranaich. The approach to Ben Lawers along this ridge is not technically difficult but is long and involves a fair amount of height gain.

Start Camusvrachan **(GR620479)**
Distance 12.1km (7½ miles)
Time 5 hours **Height gain** 1462m
Terrain steep-sided glen, high ridges, broad col, narrow main ridge
Difficulty strenuous
Popularity quiet

Route You gain Meall Choire a' Leith by climbing SW up and along the Sròn Eich. Once on the summit you follow the main ridge generally S as it winds its way to Meall Corranaich. Turn SE and descend the steep ridge to the broad col at the head of Coire Odhar. From the col, steep slopes lead SE to Beinn Ghlas – from where you follow the crest of the main Ben Lawers ridge NE to the summit.

5 MEALL GARBH ROUTE

A steep slog straight from the floor of Glen Lyon to the north ridge of Ben Lawers via the massive grassy lump of Meall Garbh.

Start Camusvrachan **(GR620479)**
Distance 9.7km (6 miles)
Time 4½ hours **Height gain** 1334m
Terrain steep slopes, high rounded ridges and craggy main ridge
Difficulty strenuous
Popularity quiet

Route The initial climb from the floor of Glen Lyon starts abruptly alongside the Allt a' Chobhair and does not relent until you reach the crest of the ridge high above Creag Roro. Once there you follow the ridge SSE to Meall Garbh, then SW across the rocky crest of An Stuc and then finally S to Ben Lawers.

6 MEALL GREIGH ROUTE

Traverses the ridge of Meall Greigh and Meall Garbh that forms a sickle shape around Lochan nan Cat and Lawers Burn.

Start A827 near Lawers **(GR680400)**
Distance 9.7km (6 miles)
Time 4½-5 hours **Height gain** 1451m
Terrain steep-sided glen, steep slopes and craggy main ridge
Difficulty strenuous
Popularity quiet

Route You gain this high-level ridge by following the good path past the farm at Machuim NNW through the ruins at East Mealour then by climbing directly N to the summit of Meall Greigh. You join the main ridge and follow it W to Meall Garbh then SW across the rocky crest of An Stuc and then finally S to Ben Lawers.

The best is yet to come! Approaching Ben Lawers.

PAUL MILLIGAN

7 LAWERS BURN ROUTE

This route follows Lawers Burn into the magnificent corrie on the east side of Ben Lawers occupied by Lochan nan Cat.

Start A827 near Lawers **(GR680400)**
Distance 6.4km (4 miles)
Time 2½-3 hours **Height gain** 1024m
Terrain steep-sided glen, steep-sided corrie, steep narrow ridge
Difficulty intermediate
Popularity quiet

Route You reach the lochan by following the good path past the farm at Machuim NNW through the ruins at East Mealour then NW and finally W. From the mouth of Lochan nan Cat turn L and climb the steep slopes S then follow the crest of the ridge SW to the summit.
Alternative: You can also gain the N ridge of Ben Lawers from Lochan nan Cat by ascending the corrie head wall at the W end of the loch. This involves some easy scrambling and joins the ridge at the col S of An Stuc.

8 SOUTH FLANK ROUTE

A quick, handy route off Ben Lawers with great views over Loch Tay – but in ascent it's a real pig!

Start A827 **(GR651379)**
Distance 2½ miles (4km)
Time 2½ hours **Height gain** 989m
Terrain steep slopes and narrow summit ridge
Difficulty strenuous
Popularity quiet

Route Steep and unremitting, this route zigzags NW from the A827 directly to the summit of Ben Lawers.

"I've climbed it"

Lawrence Brown Grimsby

A long weekend's winter walking on Ben Lawers seemed like a good idea, and I thought I'd give my six-day-old tent its first outing.

Arriving late on the Friday, we pitched the tent close to the car. We woke early next morning to the sound of rain drumming on the flysheet and our temporary home being buffeted by the wind. After breakfast, we ventured towards Ben Lawers.

As we gained height the temperature dropped, the rain turned to snow and the wind got stronger. Overmitts and balaclavas became essential as did goggles to protect eyes from the spindrift. We stopped to discuss our options: continue or retreat? The wind nearly blowing us off our feet made

the decision for us.

As we descended, the snow got harder and the cloud came in, close to white-out conditions. We found shelter, and hoped conditions would improve. They didn't. Detailed micro-navigation through the white-out was required to get back to the tent. But when we finally found it, it was in tatters. Our sleeping bags were soaked and our Trangia pans were scattered across the hill. We gathered the lot up, chucked it in the back of the car and found a Youth Hostel for the evening.

OK, so we didn't quite climb it; but the tent is repaired and the last time I looked, Ben Lawers was still there. So it's on my list of mountains to climb this year – weather permitting!

Don Bullough Wilmslow

In August 1972, the Scout troop I belonged to held its annual summer camp by Loch Lubnaig, north of Callander. It was traditional for the older Scouts to go off on a two-day expedition. The weather had been fairly mixed, but late one afternoon the weather changed for the better. The decision was made to go for it (though quite what 'it' was, we weren't too sure).

On arrival, we followed the Lawers Burn and ascended the east ridge, reaching the summit as the sun was setting. Unusually for the time of year, there was no haze and all the mountains of Scotland were visible. Well, it seemed like all of them! As the sun disappeared, we descended towards Beinn Ghlas and contoured to find a grassy spot to bivouac.

What made this trip so memorable was witnessing the sun gradually burning away the mist as we made our first brew the next morning, revealing nearby summits. We were in our own world above the clouds with the hills to ourselves. The other memory I have, is of all of us in awe of total silence.

The sight of a solitary walker appearing on the top of Beinn Ghlas signified the end of our special few hours on Ben Lawers.

LOCATION	**LAKE DISTRICT**
HEIGHT	**803m (2,634ft)**
SUMMIT GR	**273978**

Coniston Old Man

CALL HIM WHAT YOU WILL, THIS VENERABLE CHAP IS A PEOPLE MAGNET...

If you were a mountain and could claim a part in inspiring socialism, Gandhi, Proust and Tolstoy, you might think rather highly of yourself. And if you could also boast a presence not only in the southern Lakes, but also on coral reefs around the world and on the roofs of such famous institutions as the Natural History Museum, Stirling Castle and St Pancras Station, then perhaps you'd feel a tinge of pride. So when people began to call you 'Old Man', you could be excused for puffing out your chest and accepting this venerable title. Which is exactly what the Old Man of Coniston does.

The Old Man of Coniston (as he's known by the Ordnance Survey) or Coniston Old Man (according to everyone else) towers above, er, Coniston. It's one of Cumbria's more popular peaks, thanks to a combination of easy access, good paths and stunning Lakeland views. You can see Morecambe Bay from the summit on a clear day, and even Blackpool Tower. You also get one of the best possible perspectives on the Scafell range – reasons enough to recommend a mountain, you might think. But when you throw in attractions such as nearby Dow Crag (one of the best climbing and scrambling crags in the Lakes), a spectacular position as the terminal peak on the end of a ridge, great accessibility to the rest of the Coniston Fells and generally better weather than the rest of the Lakes, then you end up with a Seriously Popular Mountain. Just as a pencil museum attracts even those who can't draw, the Old Man magnetises just about every pair of boots south of the Scafell Pike divide.

Facts

Maps OS Outdoor Leisure (1:25,000) 6; OS Landranger (1:50,000) 90 & 96; Harveys Superwalker (1:25,000) Southern Lakeland & Harveys Walker (1:40,000) Southern Lakeland

Nearest town Coniston

Accommodation hotels, B&Bs, Youth Hostels (Holly How – tel. (015394) 41323, Coniston Coppermines – tel. (015394) 41261 and campsites in Coniston

Tourist information Coniston – tel. (015394) 41533

GRAHAM THOMPSON

The zigzags of the tourist route clearly show the Old Man's popularity, so why not try an alternative way?
GRAHAM THOMPSON

JEREMY ASHCROFT

From Dow Crag, the Old Man's white mane catches the sun.

It's been a popular hill for a very long time, but for changing reasons. Back in the Bronze Age folk first began to see its potential and are thought to have started the quarrying that persists to the present day. During the intervening years the Old Man has given up thousands of tons of blue and green slate – a stone now famous and exported worldwide – plus countless quantities of copper used to 'copper-bottom' wooden boats against limpets and seaweed. He's given up his forests too, to be used for housing and on hearths, but in reward now has bits of his person spread liberally around the world and particles of his carbon circulating in the upper atmosphere. But, perhaps more significantly, this Old Man of Coniston inspired the other Old Man of Coniston – the great thinker and Victorian genius John Ruskin. Ruskin lived in Coniston for almost 30 years, formulating social theories, writing, painting and generally exerting an influence on some of the great and rather intellectual men of history. But he never grew bored of the Old Man. In fact, he loved it so much he had a window specially made so he could gaze out at the lake and mountain. Who knows what Ruskin would have been without this great mountain to inspire his thoughts to greater heights...

These days, Coniston Old Man still sits there patiently, sharing his views with walkers and his rocks with the miners, shredding clouds and bathing in sunshine as the weather sees fit. And although it's tempting to personify him with an accolade like 'Old Man', possible to accuse him of pride and an over-inflated chest, and search for his influence in human thought and the great social movements of the 20th century, it's far better to not to worry about these things – and simply go climb him instead.

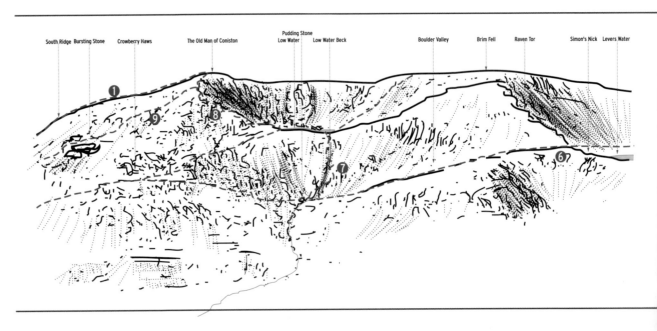

South Ridge Bursting Stone Crowberry Haws The Old Man of Coniston Pudding Stone Low Water Low Water Beck Boulder Valley Brim Fell Raven Tor Simon's Nick Levers Water

The times given are for the walk to the summit only – not there and back.

1 SOUTH RIDGE

An enjoyable route that climbs straight up the rounded crest of the south ridge. The ground is pathless once you leave the Walna Scar Road, but easy to follow; and if you are feeling adventurous there is the odd crag to scramble up if you need to get your hands on rock.

Start Coniston (GR302977)
Distance 4.8km (3 miles)
Time 2-2½ hours

Height gain 743m
Terrain open moorland and broad grassy ridge with occasional rock outcrops
Difficulty easy
Popularity quiet

Route The Walna Scar Road starts up a minor road near the Sun Hotel. Take it SW as it climbs to a car park then continue past Boo Tarn and through the rock gates to a large cairn at the start of The Cove path. Climb the grassy slope behind the cairn then at the top branch R and climb the broad ridge line N directly to the summit of The Old Man.

From Wansfell, before Head & Shoulders was invented.

2 GOAT'S HAUSE VIA THE COVE

Quiet wooded lanes, high expansive moorland and a wild craggy corrie. You get three landscapes for the price of one on this route!

Start Torver (**GR3284942**)
Distance 6.4km (4 miles)
Time 2½ hours
Height gain 695m
Terrain open moorland, high valley, steep-sided corrie, exposed col and steep fellside
Difficulty easy
Popularity moderate
Variation At the outlet of Goat's Water you can climb the steep SW flank direct; you'll encounter some easy scrambling.

Route At the side of Wilson Cottage take the lane NW then NE to Tranearth and the bridleway. Join the bridleway and follow it NW past the climbing hut at Tranearth, then past the Blue Hole at Banishead to the large cairn on the Walna Scar Road. Climb the grassy slope behind the cairn and follow The Cove path NW to Goat's Water then N to Goat's Hause. From the hause take clear path E then SE to summit of The Old Man of Coniston.

3 GOAT'S HAUSE VIA SEATHWAITE TARN

Well off the beaten track, this approach takes in some very wild country; it is nevertheless the most direct route from the Duddon Valley.

Start Seathwaite Bridge (**GR232968**)
Distance 4.25km (6¾ miles)
Time 2½ hours
Height gain 658m
Terrain open fell, high valley, reservoir, boggy corrie, exposed col and steep fellside

Difficulty intermediate
Popularity quiet

Route Take the tarmacked section of the Walna Scar Road E to the intake gate then take the reservoir access road N then E to the dam. Follow the path around N side of Seathwaite Tarn first E then S as it crosses the bogs; it then climbs steeply to Goat's Hause. From Goat's Hause take the clear path E then SE to the summit of The Old Man of Coniston.

4 CONISTON FELLS MAIN RIDGE

A superb high-level ridge walk – a real classic. The ascent from Wrynose Pass is a bit of a slog but once on the ridge the going is easy and there is little loss of height all the way to the The Old Man of Coniston.

Start Wrynose Pass (**GR277027**)
Distance 3.5km (5½ miles)
Time 2 hours
Height gain 660m
Terrain steep fellside and high mountain ridge
Difficulty easy
Popularity busy

Route From the top of Wrynose Pass climb the steep fellside SW onto Wet Side Edge. Climb Wet Side Edge to Little Carrs then turn S and follow the ridge path over Swirl How and Brim Fell to The Old Man of Coniston.

5 SWIRL HOW VIA PRISON BAND

Prison Band, the narrow ridge that links Wetherlam to the main Coniston Fells, provides an easy but exciting scramble.

Start Coniston (**GR302977**)
Distance 9.7km (6 miles)
Time 3-3½ hours
Height gain 831m
Terrain rocky valley, reservoir, boggy corrie, steep narrow ridge and high mountain ridge
Difficulty intermediate
Popularity busy
Variation You can gain Swirl Hause and Prison Band from Little Langdale by ascending W then S through Greenburn. The start is on the Little Langdale Road at **GR316034**

Route Take the minor road into the Coppermines Valley, then follow the old mines road NW up to Levers Water. Pass the dam and take the path on the E side of Levers Water N to Swirl Hause. From Swirl Hause turn L and climb the rocky crest of Prison Band W to Swirl How. From the summit cairn head S along the main ridge over Brim Fell to The Old Man of Coniston.

6 LEVERS HAUSE

You can easily gain the main ridge at Levers Hawse by an interesting path that traverses the eastern flank of Coniston Fells via Boulder Valley then an ascent through

Coniston Old Man from Swirl How.

the high, hidden corrie of Gill Cove. If you fancy a bit of bouldering the 'Pudding Stone' in Boulder Valley will provide a good hour's entertainment.

Start Coniston **(GR302977)**
Distance 6.4km (4 miles)
Time 3 hours
Height gain 883m
Terrain rocky valley, boulders, steep fell, scree and high mountain ridge
Difficulty intermediate
Popularity quiet

Route Take the minor road into the Coppermines Valley to the Miners' Bridge. Cross the bridge and join the path on the other side. Follow it W to a junction at Crowberry Haws. Take the old quarry track which contours NW then descends to the bottom of Boulder Valley. Climb N through Boulder Valley to the shoulder at Simon's Nick then skirt the W side of Levers Water. Above the western most part of Levers Water the path turns W. Follow it alongside the beck and up through Gill Cove to Levers Hawse. From here join the main path and take it S to The Old Man of Coniston.

7 BRIM FELL & LOW WATER BECK SCRAMBLES

Three hundred and fifty metres of first class scrambling. Low Water is technical and enclosed while Brim Fell is slightly easier but with more exposure.

Start Coniston **(GR303977)**
Distance 4.8km (3 miles)
Time 2½ hours
Height gain 743m
Terrain rocky valley, scramble and steep rocky corrie
Difficulty strenuous (scramble: Low Water Beck Grade 3, Brim Fell Grade 2)
Popularity quiet

Route Take the minor road into the Coppermines Valley to the Miners' Bridge. Cross the bridge and join the path on the other side. Follow it W to a junction at Crowberry Haws. Take the old quarry track which contours NW to Low Water Beck. Turn L and follow the beck to the bottom of the cleft and waterfall. Scramble up rib on R to recess then exit on R wall to a platform. From the platform continue R along diagonal rake then trend L up exposed rock and heather to a terrace. From here gain the top of the waterfall then follow the beck on RH side (as difficulties allow) to Low Water. Ascend R side of most westerly beck which flows into Low Water to foot of the broad spur. Climb this and then scramble up slabs and buttresses to a steep wall. Turn the wall on L via gully which leads onto the main ridge. From summit of Brim Fell turn S and follow good path to The Old Man of Coniston.

8 TOURIST ROUTE

If you like walking with 'the whole world and its dog', and exploring old quarry workings is your thing, then this is the route for you. If not, then leave it well alone!

Start Coniston **(GR302977)**
Distance 4km (2½ miles)
Time 2-2½ hours
Height gain 743m
Terrain rocky valley, quarries and slate-strewn ridge
Difficulty easy
Popularity busy
Variation You can also reach it via the old quarry road from the Walna Scar Road car park

Route Take the minor road to the Sun Hotel. Turn R up the lane at the side of the hotel and follow it through the farm and then NW alongside Church Beck. As path leaves Church Beck follow it W to the junction at Crowberry Haws. From the junction take the main path W as it climbs through the old quarries, past Low Water and then up the zigzags to the summit.

Tourist Route

Summit Route (winter II)
The Old Man of Coniston
Percy's Passage (winter III/V)
South Gully (winter III)
North Gully (winter III)

Low Water

JEREMY ASHCROFT

Brim Fell and Swirl How from Coniston Old Man with the Scafell massif.

It's all mine! Flasher, in Coniston Coppermines.

ASHLEY COOPER

9 BURSTING STONE ROUTE

Follows a line close to the 'tourist route', but one that is infinitely better with great views and little quarry clutter.

Start Coniston **(GR302977)**
Distance 4km (2½ miles)
Time 2-2½ hours
Height gain 743m
Terrain open moorland and steep, rocky fellside
Difficulty intermediate
Popularity moderate

Route The Walna Scar Road starts up the minor road near the Sun Hotel. Take it SW as it climbs to the car park then continue along to the quarry road turning near Boo Tarn. Just past the quarry road a vague path climbs NW up the fellside; follow it as it winds up to join the Tourist Path just below the summit of The Old Man of Coniston.

GRAHAM THOMPSON

Some girls just can't resist the charms of an Older Man....

Coniston Old Man from the east (Levers Water Beck).

"I've climbed it"

A Hodges, Plympton

Coniston Old Man holds a very special place in our hearts. As a young lad I visited Coniston Water on family day trips and remember seeing walkers in the village with big boots and vivid red, knee-length socks. How I wanted to emulate them!

Now, many years later, my wife and I have visited the top of the Old Man many times. We have walked there in summer, run over it, scrambled on it and struggled along its flanks in mountain marathons. Recently we were writing our wills and had to consider what to do with our ashes. We both suggested the Old Man's summit as our final resting place. It was our first and will be our last mountain!

Samantha Mager, Shrewsbury

The Old Man has provided me with one of my most surreal walking experiences. As the path led us up past the old quarry we noticed a dull but persistent drumming sound. We were increasingly intrigued by this as it stayed with us while we ascended, getting louder and louder. The true source of this accompaniment was only revealed to us as we reached the summit: a robed Buddhist monk was kneeling on a prayer mat gently pounding on a drum!

Valerie Lunn, Ayton

The ascent of the 'Old Man' was memorable for us as it marked the first of many 'Girls' Walking Weekends' in the Lakes. We set off on a bright late September morning in 1995 armed with basic gear and a keen sense of adventure.

With an average age of 40 years, Gill, Heather, Paula and I giggled, chattered, joked and sang – anything to take our minds off how hot and tired we were becoming. Eventually we reached the summit! The views were stunning and we were so proud of our achievement. After sharing our picnic with the sheep we started our descent. The cloud began to gather and fairly soon the Old Man disappeared into a magical mist. Weary but elated, we asked each other "Where shall we climb next?"

Getting to know you

FAMILIARITY BREEDS CONTENT. INVEST A FEW DAYS IN JUST ONE PEAK AND THE REWARDS WILL BE BOUNDLESS...

WORDS MATT SWAINE PHOTOGRAPHY TOM BAILEY AND GRAHAM THOMPSON

Wainwright's words of wisdom enlighten the **Trail Two**.

"Fingers on buzzers; here is your starter for ten. What links these three locations: Lochnagar, Hoy and Coniston?" Bzzzzzzzzzz...

If you answered 'old men' then award yourself a well-deserved pat on the back, as all three do indeed have a geriatric connection. Hoy, the second largest island in the Orkney group, has a 137m old-timer – a sandstone stack loved by climbers. Lochnagar is home to a fictional OAP immortalised in a kid's book by the Prince of Wales. But it's Coniston's Old Man that's the walker magnet. The most southerly bastion of high Lake peaks, it is a mountain that wears the ravaged lines of advancing age with dignity. Pitted and scarred by mining, its real treasure is as bountiful as ever despite generations of plunder. All you need to tap into its rich seams are a pair of boots, a map and some free time.

But if you'd asked me what that treasure was a few months ago, I'd have struggled to give you an answer. You see, the last time I set foot on its summit I just wasn't paying attention. It was over 20 years ago during a family holiday to the Lakes, and my memory of that classic ascent is a little foggy. I was at an age when my kit list consisted of a cap gun, Action Man lunch box and Star Wars action figures. I was more interested in re-enacting the moment of paternal revelation between Darth and Luke on the summit cairn than marvelling at the imposing buttresses of Dow Crag to the west. It was a terrible waste, but go easy on me... I was only nine.

Still, growing up on the south coast, hundreds of miles from England's most impressive peaks, I did squander those few chances to get to know the Lakes at an early age. And to really drive that fact home, all my recent trips have been with people who spent their childhood being shown its delights, their teens climbing its crags and their adult years walking its ridges and valleys. They are now passing that knowledge on to their children... as well as late developers like myself.

Their intimacy with this part of the UK is enviable, and I'm under no illusions; it's going to take me years to get anywhere near their encyclopaedic knowledge of the Lakes. But surely even I could emulate it on a smaller scale? By dedicating a few days to one mountain, I decided it was time to make amends for youthful indiscretions and lay the foundations for closer Lakeland relations.

Given our history, Coniston Old Man was the obvious starting point. Only this time I'd be leaving the action figures behind and enlisting the help of one of the Lakes' elder statesmen: Alfred Wainwright. His books have set thousands of walkers on the right track; but, more importantly, they offered me a model for really getting to know the hills. I was going to 'discover' the routes for myself and spend a little time with paper and pen, as he would have done: walking, sketching but most importantly taking time to absorb the hills. I was going to 'do a Wainwright'...

Of course, it's unlikely that he would have allowed himself to be talked into an introductory ascent of Dow Crag's Easter Gully. To be honest, having swung my backside over a 200ft void, I wondered if this was really a prerequisite for mountain intimacy. I had been talked into the climb by two of those enviably knowledgeable Lakes walkers, Trail's Graham Thompson and Jeremy Ashcroft. We'd picked out an easy three-pitch route, but wet weather was spicing things up a little. "You'll need to get your rock boots on for this bit," said Jeremy, belaying out of sight on the ledge above me. "The rock's really greasy." That wasn't what I

"THE CACOPHONY OF WATER ON STONE AND THE ICY CHILL OF H_2O UNDER A BLAZING SUN MADE THIS AN ASCENT TO REMEMBER..."

Scrambling up Low Water Beck has to be one of the best ways up Coniston Old Man.

wanted to hear. "Climbing," I called back, before trying to follow the moves he'd made. But hanging over this yawning void I was finding it difficult to locate the kind of handholds needed to still my legs' involuntary jitterbugging. It's at times like this that four points of contact seem positively inadequate; but, by using elbows and knees, I reckoned I could boost that to a grip-tastic eight. It would buy me some thinking time at least.

The logic for starting with a climb had seemed compellingly obvious a few hours earlier. Most people tackle their favourite hill in one of a handful of ways and if we were really going to get to know this area, we needed to break the mould. We needed to investigate every possible approach. We needed to walk away with an ascent for every occasion and a few hidden secrets, able to name the hills you can see from the summit at every point of the compass. That was the logic; but, stuck at the crux of this climb, I had other things on my mind.

With luck and just a hint of judgment I made the move, despite conflicting advice from my co-climbers, then clambered to safety gulping for air between fits of 'oh-god-I've-made-it' laughter. At the back of this voluminous ledge, I got my first good view of Coniston Old Man cloaked in mist,

Looking for routes up Boulder Valley's Pudding Stone.

Walking up from Boo Tarn to the summit of The Old Man with Dow Crag in view.

rising high above Goats Water.

Dow Crag is the yin to Coniston's elderly yang, and the network of gullies that lie between its six main buttresses are littered with the exploits of early Lakeland climbers. Dow Crag is all rocky brawn rippling over a sculpted volcanic physique, while The Old Man offers much softer approaches: a ridge to the north, grassy mounded hills to the south and a zigzagging tourist trail that winds through mining detritus to the east – which is exactly where I found myself the following day.

I'd started out early but I was still surprised to discover I had it pretty much to myself. After all, this was the bustling tourist track that Wainwright detested, but there were none of the day trippers who spoiled it for him. The '…courting couples, troops of earnest Boy Scouts, babies and grandmothers… fancy handbags and painted

45

Taking the 'tourist track' up from Low Water.

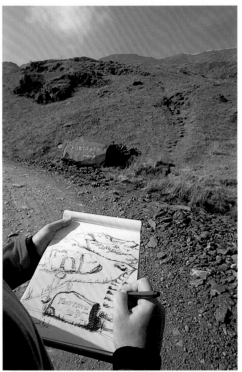

Doodling in Coppermines Valley.

"...swinging my backside over a 200ft void, I wondered if this was really a prerequisite for mountain intimacy..."

toenails…' that he'd warned of were replaced by a drizzle of ardent, well-equipped hikers.

Like me, they had chosen to tackle the most abused side of The Old Man despite the great drifts of excavated rock spilling down its eastern flanks. Mining cable stretches the length of the path and the skeletal pylons that once held them aloft lie belly-up with arms outstretched. The neat drystone buildings that dot this side of the hill house rusted furnaces and industrial museum pieces, exposed to the elements under rotting timbers and missing slate. Gaze into the damp tunnels and caves, and you find boulders the size of a small car dynamited from their ceiling sockets and plunged dagger-like into the soil below.

Yes, it's ugly – as Wainwright points out – but the stiff climb and stunning views over Coppermines Valley make it difficult to dislike. I took advantage of the oddities here to stop and investigate, sit and sketch, then stretch out on the banks of Low Water tarn to just soak up the view. It looked like it was going

to be my last today.

Sure enough, by the time I got to the summit my world had been reduced to a 10m visibility radius. I stopped to talk to a group taking their Mountain Leader assessment at the summit and on their advice decided to head to Swirl How.

Actually, I tell a lie… I'd decided to head to Dow Crag, but got my pacing wrong and missed the turning that should have taken me there via Goat's Hawse. It was only when I caught a glimpse of Levers Water through a break in the clag that I realised where I was. Still, I was here to explore; and 'lost' is rather a relative term. What's more, every now and again straying from your intended path can lead you directly to points of real interest.

"Have you seen the World War Two bomber wreckage up towards Great Carrs?" asked another walker as I reached the Swirl How cairn. "Follow that path for about 400 yards and you should find it, even in this weather!" Sure enough a cairn, cross and aircraft undercarriage mark the spot where Halifax

LL505 S-Sugar hit the ground on 22 October 1944 with the loss of eight lives. It's odd to think of the war touching this quiet corner of the Lakes, but almost 60 years later this memorial acts as a poignant reminder of the crew's sacrifice.

Firmly back on track, I headed down the Prison Band and past Levers Water, then spent that afternoon and the following morning looking for scrambling routes on Raven Tor and Low Water Beck, or sketching and climbing the rocks in Boulder Valley. With the sun shining the river sprang into life with insects and birds rushing to meet their procreational deadlines. High on the ridges delinquent ravens (probably with armed with flick-knives) mobbed any buzzard foolish enough to glide into their airspace.

I could have stayed there all afternoon but I'd planned to meet Tom and Piers from Trail HQ back in Coniston. We were going to walk the circular route from the Walna Scar Road up Coniston Old Man to Dow Crag and back down.

We picked up the path by Boo Tarn quite easily and lost it just as effortlessly as it led us over the series of grassy mounds that make up The Old Man's southern face. There are still reminders of the mining industry here and Bursting Stone Quarry looks far worse than anything on the eastern side because it's set in untouched surroundings. But this was Wainwright's favourite route up, which he described as: "…a succession of fascinating and unexpected zigzags making use of grassy terraces scented with thyme and tiny alpines…" It's a climb that keeps you in suspense too, making you wait until the summit for a view of Dow Crag, the Scafells and Great End. "I reckon you can see the whole of Lakeland from here," exclaimed Piers as we hit the top. "Makes you realise just how small it is," added Tom. Perhaps discovering the Lakes wasn't going to be such a tall order after all.

The view on the other side of Goat's Water soon set me straight. Looking down into the monstrous gullies of Dow Crag I realised that there was a year's-worth of climbing here alone. It was the view from Dow Crag that afternoon that brought our day to a close. As the sun set, the Isle of Man seemed to be hovering like Cloud City above a pastel sea of pink vapour.

The following morning found us playing on the Pudding Stone, Boulder Valley's resident bad boy. Wainwright reckoned it was 'as large as a house', and it offers some entertaining bouldering or an easy walk up if you've left your rock boots at home. From the top, looking towards The Old Man, the first thing you see is the riotous cascade of Low Water Beck falls, where the water plummets 150m from its eponymous tarn. This holds a Grade 3 scramble, one of the best in this area and the cacophony of water on stone and the icy chill of H2O under a blazing sun made this an ascent to remember. It's easy enough to avoid a soaking as you hop from one side of the bank to the other, but it's much more fun to risk it every now and again. It's exhilarating and exposed which is why, thoroughly soaked at the other end of our scramble, we slumped next to the Mediterranean blue of Low Water.

After four days on Coniston Old Man, I would urge you to try this route up above all others… and it's a nice feeling being able to pass on that sort of recommendation. Taking time to get to know this mountain means, in a very small way, I've made it my own. It's a corner of the Lakes that I will treasure, but it's far from 'ticked off'. Searching through guidebooks, I've already found a couple of scrambles that I missed, including one that leads from Low Water up Brim Fell – a favourite of Coniston Tiger Harry Griffin – and I've no doubt there are hundreds of others to investigate. To really get to know it I need to book a trip in the height of summer and the depths of winter, to spend a few nights camping out or sleeping in the bivvy spots we found; and then there are a host of climbs waiting to be tackled and good mountain days to be had.

So if there's a little bit of the Lakes, a part of the Peaks, a wedge of Wales or a slice of Scotland that you are dying to get to know, invest some time in discovering its secrets. Hunt out a guide book and find those routes you've yet to walk, dig for little-known treasures, use the backwater paths and ignored ways up. Take time to look around: make it your own.

Looking out towards the Isle of Man from Dow Crag.

Old acquaintance

Coniston Old Man's nooks and crannies, at a glance…

ILLUSTRATIONS **JEREMY ASHCROFT**

DOW CRAG

This is simply one of the best climbing spots in the Lakes. So pick up a copy of Dow, Duddon and Slate by A Phizacklea, pb FRCC 1993, distributed by Cordee – tel. (0116) 254 3579.

[Map showing Coniston Old Man area with labels: Grey Friar, Great Carrs, Swirl How, AIRCRAFT CRASH SITE, Prison Band, Wetherlam, RIDGE WALK, Levers Hause, Swirl Hause, Seathwaite Tarn, Brim Fell, SCRAMBLE, Raven Tor, Levers Water, HORSESHOE WALK, Dow Crag, Goat's Hawse, RED DELL, CLIMB, Old Man of Coniston, Low Water, SCRAMBLE, Low Water Beck, Buck Pike, Pudding Stone, COPPER MINES VALLEY, Brown Pike, Blind Tarn, Boulder Valley, YHA, Walna Scar, Bursting Stone Quarry, The Bell, The Cove, LITTLE ARROW MOOR, OVERNIGHT YHA, Cove Bridge, Rock Gates, Boo Tarn, Banishead Quarry, Coniston, Tranearth, Bowmanstead, NORTH]

Maps OS Outdoor Leisure (1:25,000) 6; OS Landrangers (1:50,000) 90 & 96; Harvey's Superwalker (1:25,000) and Walker (1:40,000) Western Lakeland

PUDDING STONE

"The most massive and most prominent of the boulders [in Boulder Valley] is the Pudding Stone," writes Wainwright, "25 feet high and as big as a house, with a dozen climbing routes." We spent a morning trying to tackle some difficult problems on this rock. Pack your rock boots and take some time out to try them.

AIRCRAFT CRASH SITE

At 8.20pm on 22 October 1944, Halifax bomber LL505 S-Sugar, in nearly level flight from the NE, first touched ground with the port outer propeller tip at GR749237 approximately 50ft below the summit of Great Carrs at an elevation of 2,250ft. Flying Officer Jack Johnston attempted to avoid hitting the ground by pulling the nose up but the fuselage skidded over the ground for 60 yards before breaking up and burning. All eight crew members (seven Canadian and one British) lost their lives. The memorial is clearly visible from the path.

COPPER MINES

Extraction of copper on Coniston Old Man probably dates back to Roman times, but the really prosperous period for Coniston was between 1850 and 1870. Using gunpowder, drilling by hand, and with only candles for light, it would have been painfully slow work extracting the copper. Some of the mines were 1,100ft below the surface (and therefore 500ft below sea-level). These caves are dangerous places... so do not go in unless you're being taken by an experienced guide.

LOW WATER BECK SCRAMBLE

For our money, this is simply the most exhilarating way to get to the top of Coniston Old Man. Get a copy of 50 Best Scrambles In The Lake District by Bill O'Connor, pb David & Charles, which gives a full description of this and many other scrambles in the area.

Pillar

TALL TALES THREATEN TO OVERSHADOW THIS MOUNTAIN'S HANDSOME HIGH CRAGS...

WORDS MARIA DEL CARMEN CLEGG

I t's been said that Pillar is a mountain fit for nothing but ravens, sheep and climbers. While the sentiments behind this arch generalisation might well strike a chord with anyone who has ever grappled with the dubious friction properties of wet Lakeland rock, such a sweeping statement requires some investigation.

Irony can be held at least partly responsible and there is a rich tradition of leg-pulling in Wasdale. Auld Will Ritson, the first landlord of the Wasdale Head Inn, used to boast proudly that Wasdale was the home of England's highest mountain – Scafell Pike; its deepest lake – Wast Water; its smallest church; and its biggest liar – Will Ritson himself. His notoriety as a teller of preposterous tall tales spread so far in the mid-19th century that he became almost as popular a tourist attraction as the Lake District's newly discovered charms.

A somewhat more contemporary authority on the western fells, Alfred Wainwright, pointed out that Pillar itself is hardly pillar-shaped. Pillar mountain is a massif made up of buttresses and crags, and is in fact named after an outcrop on its northern flank, Pillar Rock, which Wainwright called 'the most handsome crag in Lakeland'.

Pillar and Ennerdale from Brandreth.

IAN EVANS

Facts

Maps OS Outdoor Leisure (1:25,000) 4 & 6; OS Landranger (1:50,000) 89; Harveys Superwalker (1:25,000) & Walker (1:40,000) Western Lakeland

Nearest towns Ravenglass, Gosforth

Accommodation Youth Hostel – tel. (019467) 26222 and campsites in Wasdale

Tourist information Whitehaven – tel. (01946) 852939

51

High on Pillar Rock with Ennerdale far below.

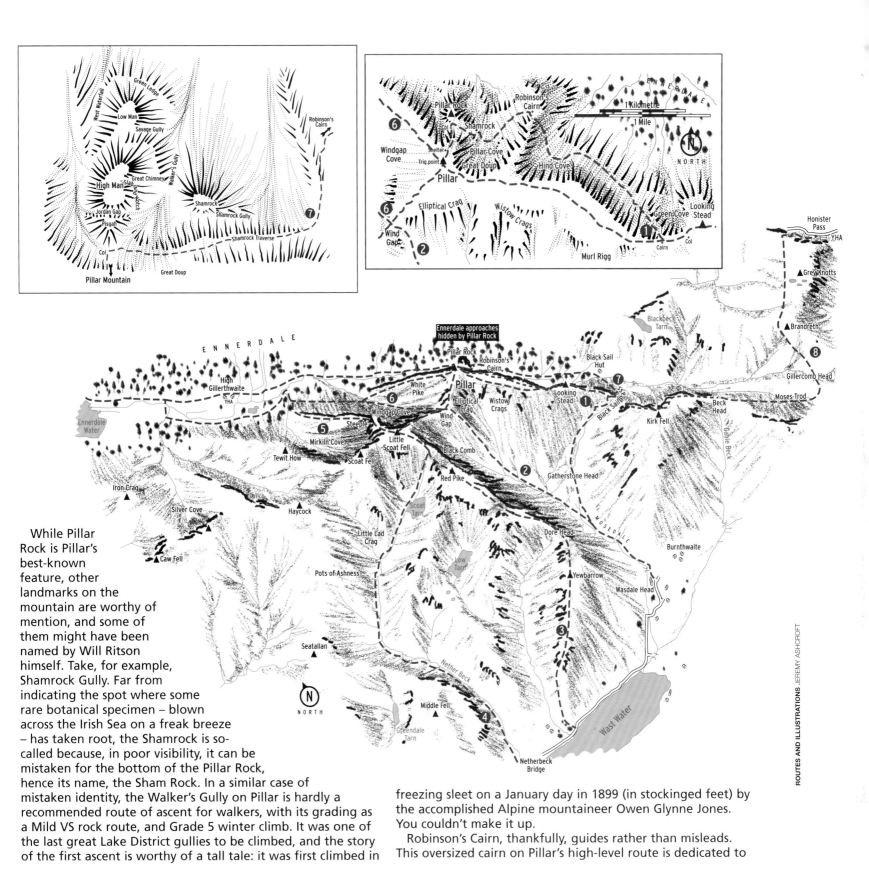

ROUTES AND ILLUSTRATIONS JEREMY ASHCROFT

While Pillar Rock is Pillar's best-known feature, other landmarks on the mountain are worthy of mention, and some of them might have been named by Will Ritson himself. Take, for example, Shamrock Gully. Far from indicating the spot where some rare botanical specimen – blown across the Irish Sea on a freak breeze – has taken root, the Shamrock is so-called because, in poor visibility, it can be mistaken for the bottom of the Pillar Rock, hence its name, the Sham Rock. In a similar case of mistaken identity, the Walker's Gully on Pillar is hardly a recommended route of ascent for walkers, with its grading as a Mild VS rock route, and Grade 5 winter climb. It was one of the last great Lake District gullies to be climbed, and the story of the first ascent is worthy of a tall tale: it was first climbed in freezing sleet on a January day in 1899 (in stockinged feet) by the accomplished Alpine mountaineer Owen Glynne Jones. You couldn't make it up.

Robinson's Cairn, thankfully, guides rather than misleads. This oversized cairn on Pillar's high-level route is dedicated to

GRAHAM THOMPSON

Steeple from Pillar, across Wind Gap.

the memory of one John Wilson Robinson, a 19th century climber and fell-walker, and one of the earliest explorers to be taken with Pillar's rugged charms. Whatever your feelings about the placing of permanent memorials in wild places, it's a useful waymarker on Pillar, not always the easiest mountain to find your way on.

Adventurous walkers with a head for heights will love this mountain, with its distinctly wild atmosphere and dizzying views. The north face is as wild and forbidding as any Lakeland peak, and Pillar Rock is the only separate Lakes top requiring climbing skills in ascent.

For that matter, all the aspects of Pillar are either impressively craggy faces or rough boulder-strewn corries, ensuring that whether you approach the mountain from Wasdale, Ennerdale or Buttermere, an ascent of Pillar is always hard-won. Which means that any tall tales you find yourself telling at the end of a day on Pillar might have at least a grain of truth in them.

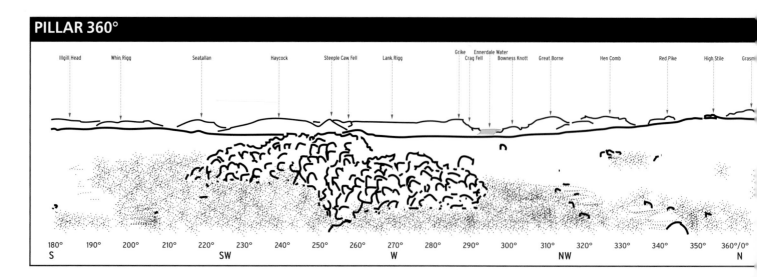

PILLAR 360°

Illgill Head — Whin Rigg — Seatallan — Haycock — Steeple Caw Fell — Lank Rigg — Grike / Crag Fell — Ennerdale Water / Bowness Knott — Great Borne — Hen Comb — Red Pike — High Stile — Grasmi

| 180° S | 190° | 200° | 210° | 220° SW | 230° | 240° | 250° | 260° | 270° W | 280° | 290° | 300° | 310° NW | 320° | 330° | 340° | 350° | 360°/0° N |

From Pillar: Gable and the Scafells, up to their chins in a cloud inversion.

IAN EVANS

the routes

● The times given are for the walk to the summit only – not there and back.

1 MOSEDALE/BLACK SAIL ROUTE

The classic approach to Pillar from Wasdale Head following the well-graded Black Sail bridleway then the crest of Pillar's south-east ridge with superb views of Pillar Rock.

Start Wasdale Head **(GR187088)**
Distance 6km (3¾ miles)
Time 2½ hours
Height gain 872m
Terrain steep-sided valley, hanging corrie, high pass, broad ridge and summit plateau
Difficulty intermediate
Popularity moderate

Variation On the W side of Looking Stead col a cairn marks the start of the high-level route. This is the climbers' approach to Pillar Rock and makes an interesting route for walkers keen to get a closer look at Pillar Rock's superb crags. It is exposed in places (particularly on the Shamrock traverse) but the scrambling is easy and should not present too many problems in clear weather.

Route From the Wasdale Head Hotel take the Black Sail bridleway NNW then N up through Mosedale. It steepens considerably towards Gatherstone Head and turns NE then E to gain the main ridge at Black Sail Pass. From the top of the pass turn L and follow the main ridge path N then W over Looking Stead. Cross the col on the W side of Looking Stead and climb generally WNW following the path around the edge of the crags to Pillar's summit plateau.

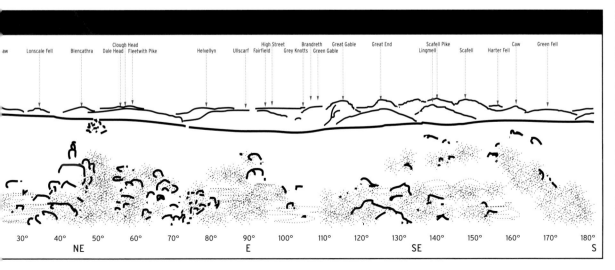

| aw | Lonscale Fell | Blencathra | Clough Head Dale Head Fleetwith Pike | Helvellyn | Ullscarf Fairfield | High Street Grey Knotts Green Gable | Brandreth Great Gable | Great End | Scafell Pike Lingmell | Scafell | Harter Fell | Caw | Green Fell |

30°　40°　50°　60°　70°　80°　90°　100°　110°　120°　130°　140°　150°　160°　170°　180°
　　NE　　　　　　　　　　　　E　　　　　　　　　　　SE　　　　　　　　　　　S

2 MOSEDALE/ WINDGAP PATH

Short and steep, this route is the quickest way up and down Pillar.

Start Wasdale Head **(GR187088)**
Distance 4km (2½ miles)
Time 2- 2½ hours
Height gain 812m
Terrain steep-sided valley, hanging corrie, exposed col, broad ridge and summit plateau
Difficulty strenuous
Popularity quiet

Route From the Wasdale Head Hotel take the Black Sail bridleway NNW then N up through Mosedale. A path forks L from the bridleway as it starts to steepen to the gate below Gatherstone Head. Join the path and follow it NW as it climbs the head wall of Mosedale to gain the col at Wind Gap. From Wind Gap turn NE and climb the steep broad ridge onto the SW side of Pillar's summit plateau.

3 YEWBARROW PATH

Climbs the steep, well-defined south-west ridge of Yewbarrow to gain Pillar by crossing Dore Head and ascending Red Pike and Little Scoat Fell. Forms the western half of the Mosedale Horseshoe – a superb outing.

Start Bowderdale car park **(GR168068)**
Distance 7km (4½ miles)
Time 3-3½ hours
Height gain 1118m
Terrain steep ridge, high col, high mountain ridge, exposed col, broad ridge and summit plateau
Difficulty strenuous
Popularity moderate

Route Climb straight up Yewbarrow's south-west ridge past Dropping Crag direct to the top then descend NNE along the crest to Dore Head.
Cross the col NW and make the steep ascent to Red Pike. Head NW from Red Pike to gain the main ridge at Little Scoat Fell. Turn ENE and follow the path to Wind Gap then make the final ascent NE to Pillar.

4 NETHER BECK PATH

A long, steady approach alongside the waters of Nether Beck then gaining the western side of the Pillar massif via the superbly situated corrie occupied by Scoat Tarn.

Start Lakeside road near Netherbeck Bridge **(GR159063)**
Distance 7.5km (4¾ miles)
Time 3 hours
Height gain 918m

Black Sail Youth Hostel, on route 7.

TOM BAILEY

Terrain steep-sided valley, hanging corrie, exposed col, broad ridge and summit plateau
Difficulty intermediate
Popularity quiet

Route From the road follow the Nether Beck bridleway (vague at first) up the W side of Nether Beck to a junction at the head of the valley. Take the R fork and follow it NE as it climbs to Scoat Tarn. Continue NE along the NW side of the tarn and climb to the col on the N side of Red Pike. Turn L and climb NW to Little Scoat Fell. Turn ENE and follow the path to Wind Gap then make the final ascent NE to Pillar.

5 NORTH RIDGE OF STEEPLE

A rewarding route that climbs an elegant line directly up the crest of the north ridge of Steeple. It rises steeply out of Ennerdale and gets you into some superb situations particularly near the top where you can look out over the eastern crags into the depths of Mirk Cove.

Start Bowness car park **(GR101153)**
Distance 9.3km (5¾ miles)
Time 3½ hours
Height gain 877m
Terrain long forested valley, river, woodland, steep mountainside, narrow ridge, high mountain ridge, exposed col, broad ridge and summit plateau
Difficulty strenuous
Popularity quiet

Route Follow the bridleway (forest track) ESE along Ennerdale to cross the River Liza at the footbridge near the Woundell Beck confluence. Then follow the footpath on the S side of the River Liza E to cross Low Beck. Just after crossing

the beck turn R and climb S to gain the open fell at the base of the north ridge of Steeple. Climb the crest of the ridge directly to the summit of Steeple. Continue S over Steeple then turn SE to gain the main ridge at Little Scoat Fell. Turn ENE and follow the path to Wind Gap then make the final ascent NE to Pillar.

6 WINDGAP COVE ROUTE

Explores the high remote Windgap Cove on the west side of Pillar – safe descent route back to Ennerdale.

Start Bowness car park **(GR101153)**
Distance 8.2km (5 miles)
Time 3 hours
Height gain 776m
Terrain long forested valley, river, woodland, steep mountainside, open corrie, exposed col, broad ridge and summit plateau
Difficulty intermediate
Popularity quiet

Variation Instead of climbing up through Windgap Cove, you can follow the bounding N edge of the corrie (Pillar's north-west ridge) instead.

Route Follow the bridleway (forest track) ESE along Ennerdale to cross the River Liza at the footbridge near the Woundell Beck confluence. Then follow the footpath on the S side of the River Liza E to cross Low Beck. Just after crossing the beck turn R and climb S up through the trees to a junction at the 220m contour mark. Take the path that forks L and follow it SE up into Windgap Cove. Climb up through the corrie to reach Wind Gap then make the final ascent NE to Pillar.

7 ENNERDALE/ BLACK SAIL PASS ROUTE

Simple, handy route if you are staying at Black Sail Youth Hostel.

Start Black Sail Youth Hostel **(GR195124)** or Bowness car park **(GR101153)**
Distance 4km (2½ miles)
Time 2 hours
Height gain 652m
Terrain steep-sided valley, steep corrie, high pass, broad ridge and summit plateau
Difficulty intermediate
Popularity moderate

Route From Black Sail Youth Hostel follow the bridleway SE, S then SW as it climbs steeply to the top of Black Sail Pass. From here turn R and follow the main ridge path N the W over Looking Stead. Cross the col on the W side of Looking Stead and climb generally WNW following the path around the edge of the crags to Pillar's summit plateau.

8 MOSES TROD/HIGH-LEVEL ROUTE

A long, intricate approach from Honister Pass via a devious course along Moses Trod then, after skirting Kirk Fell, along the high-level route (climber's approach to Pillar Rock).

Start Honister Pass **(GR225135)**
Distance 10km (6¼ miles)
Time 3-3½ hours
Height gain 673m
Terrain steep mountainsides, valley heads, scree, high pass, broad ridge, summit plateau
Difficulty strenuous
Popularity quiet

Route From the top of Honister Pass climb the bridleway W to the broad col on the S side of Fleetwith Pike. Then take Moses Trod (path) S as it skirts the W flank of Grey Knotts, Brandreth and Green Gable. It turns W under the north face of Great Gable to reach the col at Beck Head. At Beck Head leave Moses Trod to follow the path that descends NW then levels and traverses past Kirk Fell under Boat How Crags up to Black Sail Pass.

From Black Sail Pass follow the main ridge path NW then W over Looking Stead to the col on the W side. Continue a short way W on the other side of the col to a cairn marking the start of the high-level route. Follow the high-level path as it traverses through Green Cove and Hind Cove to Robinson's Cairn.

From the cairn continue on the path as it descends slightly W then climbs SW towards Shamrock. Before the base of Shamrock the path hits a low rock bluff which it ascends to gain a scree slope, and after a short ascent of this it reaches the start of a terrace – this is the Shamrock Traverse. Follow this airy traverse easily to a rough col on the S side of Pisgah. From the col climb the rocky ridge steeply S to the summit plateau of Pillar.

"I've climbed it"

Jennifer Hynes, Rawtenstall

It was May 2000, and we had a week in Coniston. Every day had been cold, miserable and windy, and this day showed no signs of being any different. Regardless, we drove to Wast Water and set off up to the Black Sail Pass. Pillar loomed under a menacing black sky, but we weren't deterred! At the top of the pass we turned up to the summit which took us over grassy patches broken by some scrambling terrain, offering views down to Ennerdale valley, which looked even more spectacular with bright sunny patches.

The flat summit was home to a cheeky sheep with its lamb who wanted to pinch our food (tough!). We moved up to Windy Gap for a peaceful (and not too windblown) lunch before setting off for Black Crag, Steeple and Red Pike.

The panoramic views on this part of our walk were fantastic and with the sky clear and the sun blazing, we could see forever. We felt justified in dumping our gear and ourselves on the grassy verge above Low Tarn to bask in bliss for an hour. Finally we walked along the edge of Yewbarrow to the road, where Wast Water rippled and glistened peacefully, and on to the inn for the customary pint. Perfect!

Mick Jury, Barrow-in-Furness

I doubt I will ever forget my first time on Pillar Rock. I had climbed Pillar many times before by most of the ascent routes, and this was to be the day we attempted the Slab and Notch route on Pillar Rock.

One of our trio didn't fancy the scramble and stayed guarding the bags while the two of us ventured forth.

When we finally reached the top of Pillar Rock and stopped for the photo shoot, we experienced a real feeling of triumph. However the most unforgettable part of the day was still to come. As we continued on to Pillar itself, then Red Pike, my scrambling partner suffered a heart attack on the descent to Wasdale, and the next time I saw him was in the High Dependency Unit of the local hospital; fortunately he is now back to full health and back in action again!

LOCATION	LAKE DISTRICT
HEIGHT	873m (2863ft)
SUMMIT GR	358117

Fairfield

More of a massif than a mountain, Fairfield has justifiably earned a reputation among hill-walkers as one of the Lake District's finest fell days.

The view from St Sunday Crag to the sunbathing bulk of Fairfield.
GRAHAM THOMPSON

Facts

Maps OS Outdoor Leisure (1:25,000) 5 & 7; OS Landranger (1:50,000) 90; Harveys Superwalker (1:25,000) Lakeland Central

Nearest town Ambleside

Accommodation Youth Hostels in Ambleside – tel. (015394) 32304; Grasmere – tel. (015394) 35316; and Patterdale – tel. (017684) 82394; plus B&Bs, hotels and campsites

Tourist information Ambleside – tel. (015394) 32582; Grasmere – tel. (015394) 35245 and Glenridding – tel. (017684) 82414

While we wouldn't go so far as to say Fairfield has a split personality, it is a mountain whose intricate character benefits from closer inspection. Without seeing it from all sides you'll come away short-changed and with an incomplete picture that only a return visit can remedy.

Its imposing position in the Lake District only contributes to its conflicting image. Chamonix has Mont Blanc, Zermatt has the Matterhorn and Fort William has Ben Nevis. Ambleside, that giftshop-strewn village in the centre of the Lakes, is dominated by the formidable presence of Fairfield, and it is this tea-and-cake-fuelled view that lasts in the memory. Fairfield rises to the north, filling the skyline and giving an impression of real size. It's pleasant on the eye – perhaps too pleasant – and appears smooth, rounded and grassy. Its obvious altitude and the accessible ridges which tail off southwards forming a near-perfect horseshoe ensure its slopes receive plenty of bootprints.

The Fairfield Horseshoe is a well-known Lakeland classic which should be in every fell-walker's repertoire. As circular walks go, this Ambleside to Rydal round is an absolute gem – undulating over high fells with outstanding views down Windermere and out to Morecambe Bay. Yet, despite its obvious merits, it doesn't tell the whole story.

You could walk over Fairfield's rocky plateau summit every day of your life and still not know the real mountain. To become truly acquainted you need to leave the hustle and bustle of Ambleside and head north over the Kirkstone Pass and down to Brothers Water and Patterdale. It is from here that the steep and slightly claustrophobic valleys of Dovedale and Deepdale draw your eye up to the dark and imposing crags that guard Fairfield's lesser known northern and eastern approaches.

Fairfield looks and feels a different proposition from this angle, with the heads of Dovedale and Deepdale seemingly blocked by impressive sheets of rock and scree like Greenhow End, Hutaple Crag and Scrubby Crag which are almost the equal of Helvellyn's eastern reaches. These harbour impressive low- and mid-grade rock climbs; but the inquisitive walker and scrambler, however, will find gaps in the defences which lead enjoyably to the higher reaches of the mountain.

The head of Dovedale also hides a place to lay your head, if you're feeling adventurous. In the 1950s the famous Lakeland mountaineer Harry Griffin discovered a cave on Dove Crag which is a top-class bivvy site boasting views down towards Ullswater and the distant Pennines. It can sleep a dozen people, has a low wall across the front to keep the elements out and now features a visitors' book to chronicle the tales of hardy walkers and climbers who stay there.

Once on Fairfield's broad, flat summit you're shown a who's who of Lake District peaks – but it's no place to linger in bad weather. Its lack of features makes beating a hasty retreat in clag, particularly from the eastern side, an interesting proposition; and you need to be sure of your compass skills if you're to stop yourself straying down the wrong ridge. Many people have ended up in Patterdale instead of Ambleside, and vice versa!

In winter the summit plateau holds a fair amount of snow, and, as it is often blasted by wind, it can be a frozen sheet of ice requiring crampons just to stay upright, so don't be fooled by conditions in the valleys.

Whichever side of Fairfield you plan to do next time you're in the Lakes, take an extra day and try it from the other side as well – because you'll find that the opposites of this fine mountain are the attraction.

GRAHAM THOMPSON

Fairfield in its winter attire, from Hart Crag.

FAIRFIELD 360° PANORAMA

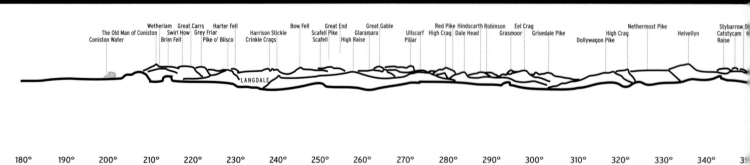

The Old Man of Coniston · Wetherlam · Great Carrs · Harter Fell · Bow Fell · Great End · Great Gable · Red Pike · Hindscarth Robinson · Eel Crag · Nethermost Pike · Stybarrow D
Coniston Water · Swirl How · Grey Friar · Harrison Stickle · Scafell Pike · Glaramara · Ullscarf · High Crag · Dale Head · Grasmoor · Grisedale Pike · High Crag · Helvellyn · Catstycam
Brim Fell · Pike o' Blisco · Crinkle Crags · Scafell · High Raise · Pillar · Dollywagon Pike · Raise

LANGDALE

| 180° | 190° | 200° | 210° | 220° | 230° | 240° | 250° | 260° | 270° | 280° | 290° | 300° | 310° | 320° | 330° | 340° | 3 |
| S | | | | SW | | | | | W | | | | NW | | | | |

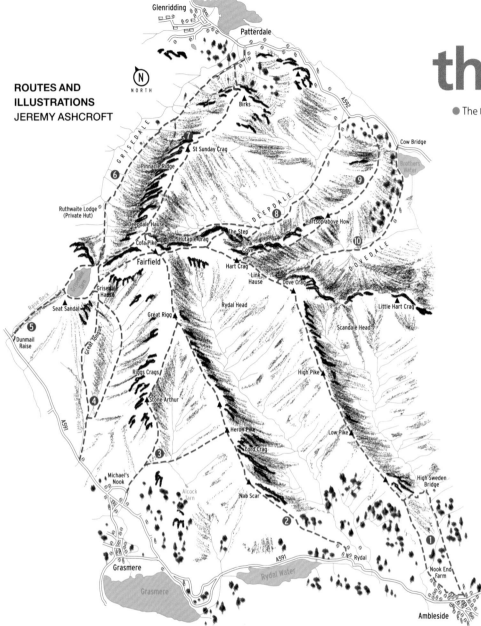

the routes

● The times given are for the walk to the summit only – not there and back.

1 HIGH PIKE RIDGE

Climbs directly from Ambleside via airy crest of the Low Pike/High Pike ridge to gain the eastern side of Fairfield's summit plateau.
Forms the eastern side of the classic Fairfield Horseshoe.

Start Ambleside (GR376046)
Distance 6.3km (4 miles)
Time 3 hours
Height gain 923m
Terrain steep fellside, rounded ridge and stony summit plateau
Difficulty intermediate
Variation you can also gain the ridge S of Low Pike via a steep ascent from High Sweden Bridge
Popularity busy

Route From the centre of Ambleside follow the lanes N to Nook End Farm. Continue N and climb the crest of the rounded ridge first over Low Pike then over High Pike to the summit of Dove Crag. Turn NW and follow the main path to Hart Crag then continue along it as it swings W to the summit of Fairfield.

2 SOUTH RIDGE

Steady climb up the great south ridge of Fairfield with superb views over Grasmere and the Central Fells. This forms the western side of the classic Fairfield Horseshoe.

Start Rydal, A591 (GR364061)
Distance 6km (3¾ miles)
Time 2½ hours
Height gain 833m
Terrain steep fellside, rounded ridge and stony summit plateau
Difficulty intermediate
Popularity busy

Route From the A591 follow the lane N through Rydal village then climb the footpath NW over Nab Scar to gain the bottom of the South Ridge. Follow the crest of the ridge N first over Heron Pike then over Great Rigg to Fairfield's summit.

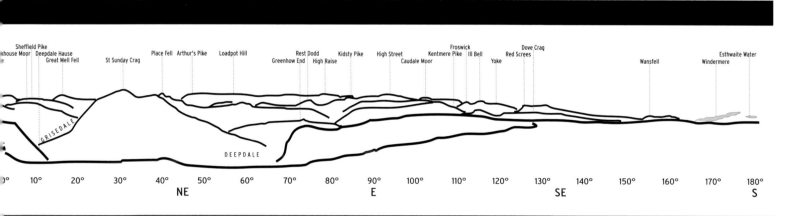

3 GRASMERE PATHS

Start Grasmere, A591 **(GR340082)**
Distance 4km (2½ miles)
Time 2 hours
Height gain 838m
Terrain steep fellside, truncated spur, rounded ridge and stony summit plateau
Difficulty intermediate
Popularity moderate
Variation steep climb E direct to the summit of Heron Pike on the south ridge

Route Follow the lanes NE through Michael's Nook then climb E then N up footpaths to the summit of Stone Arthur. Follow the crest of the Stone Arthur spur NE to gain the south ridge which you follow N to the summit of Fairfield.

4 GREAT TONGUE ROUTE

Gains the desolate Grisedale Hause via the twin ghylls of the Great Tongue then climbs the steep west ridge of Fairfield direct to the summit.

Start Mill Bridge, A591 **(GR336092)**
Distance 4.5km (2¾ miles)
Time 2 hours
Height gain 772m
Terrain steep-sided valley, steep fellside, hanging corrie, steep rounded ridge and stony summit plateau
Difficulty strenuous
Popularity moderate
Variation you can follow Tongue Gill directly to Grisedale Hause

Route From Mill Bridge follow the steep bridleway NE up the W side of the Great Tongue to the bleak col of Grisedale Hause. From the col climb steeply E up the rounded ridge to the summit of Fairfield.

5 DUNMAIL RAISE ROUTE

Shortest and most direct route to Fairfield's summit which involves the least height gain.

Start Dunmail Raise **(GR327117)**
Distance 4km (2½ miles)
Time 2-2½ hours
Height gain 635m
Terrain steep-sided ghyll, broad col, steep rounded ridge and stony summit plateau
Difficulty strenuous
Popularity moderate

Route From the A591 follow the steep path E alongside Raise Beck to the broad col by Grisedale Tarn. Follow the indistinct path around the S side of Grisedale Tarn to Grisedale Hause. From the col climb steeply E up the rounded ridge to the summit of Fairfield.

6 GRISEDALE ROUTE

A long valley approach with a steep finish up the NW flank of Fairfield.

Start Grisedale Bridge, Patterdale **(GR391161)**
Distance 7km (4½ miles)
Time 2½-3 hours
Height gain 726m
Terrain steep-sided valley, hanging corrie, steep rounded ridge and stony summit plateau
Difficulty strenuous
Popularity moderate

Rockin' along the path from Deepdale Hause.

Route From Grisedale Bridge follow the road then the bridleway SW the length of Grisedale to the outlet of Grisedale Tarn. Cross the beck then follow the steep path NNE to Deepdale Hause then SSW to the summit plateau of Fairfield.

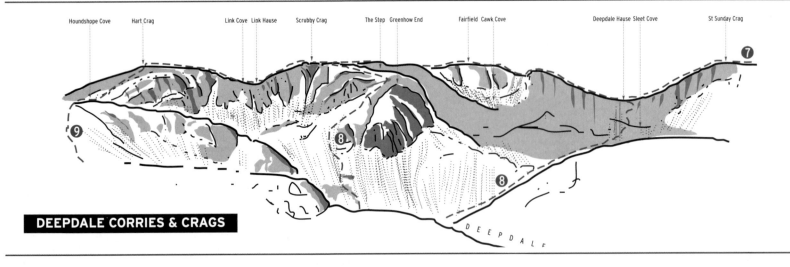

DEEPDALE CORRIES & CRAGS

Fairfield's better side – looking
up Deepdale from Angle Tarn.
TOM BAILEY

7 ST SUNDAY CRAG ROUTE (PINNACLE RIDGE)

Pinnacle Ridge is one of the best scrambles in the UK and should not be missed if you are happy climbing Grade 3 – if not you can duck out by following St Sunday Crag over Birks.

Start Grisedale Bridge, Patterdale (**GR391161**)
Distance 6km (7¼ miles)
Time 3-4 hours
Height gain 977m
Terrain steep-sided valley, steep fellside, scree, steep arête, rounded summit ridge, exposed col, narrow summit ridge and stony summit plateau
Difficulty very strenuous (Grade 3 scramble, Grade 2 winter climb)
Popularity quiet
Variation From Grisedale Bridge follow the lane 250m SW then the footpath S over Birks to gain the main ridge of St Sunday Crag

Route From Grisedale Bridge follow the road then the bridleway SW along Grisedale to the W end of Elm How Plantation. Climb SE up zigzags, then traverse SW below the crags of St Sunday Crag. Pinnacle Ridge is the most jagged ridge, with a deep gully to its R. Climb this to the summit of St Sunday Crag then descend SW to Deepdale Hause. From the col climb the narrow ridge SSW to the summit of Fairfield.

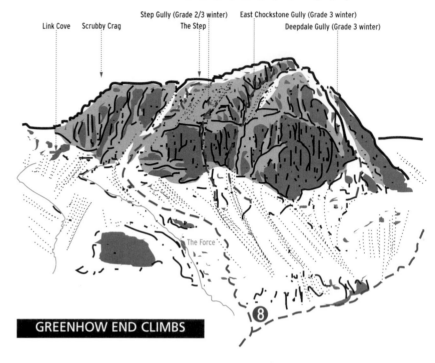

GREENHOW END

Link Cove · Scrubby Crag · Step Gully (Grade 2/3 winter) · The Step · East Chockstone Gully (Grade 3 winter) · Deepdale Gully (Grade 3 winter)

The Force

⑧

GREENHOW END CLIMBS

Taking the long view of Fairfield, from Loughrigg Fell.

GRAHAM THOMPSON

8 DEEPDALE PATH

A trek into the depths of one of Lakeland's wild corners.

Start Bridgend (**GR399143**)
Distance 5.5km (3½ miles)
Time 2½-3 hours
Height gain 714m
Terrain rough steep-sided valley, hanging corrie, exposed col, narrow summit ridge and stony summit plateau
Difficulty strenuous
Popularity quiet
Variation From the head of Deepdale, cross Mossydale to the base of the waterfalls cascading from Link Cove. A Grade 3 scramble then leads up the LH waterfall to Link Cove. Walk R to the obvious crags of Greenhow End and scramble over these to join the main ridge. Turn W to the summit of Fairfield.

Route From Bridgend take the track W then SW to Deepdale Hall. Past the hall continue SW and follow the Deepdale Path through the valley to make the steep climb to Deepdale Hause. From the col climb the narrow ridge SSW to the summit of Fairfield.

9 HARTSOP ABOVE HOW PATH

A long sweeping ridge with superb all-round views – not to be missed.

Start Bridgend **(GR399143)**
Distance 6.2km (3¾ miles)
Time 2½ hours
Height gain 789m
Terrain woodland, steep rounded ridge, stony summit plateau
Difficulty intermediate
Popularity moderate

Route From Bridgend follow the path S through woodland to gain the Hartsop path above How Path. Follow it along the crest of the ridge SSW then SW to the summit of Hart Crag. From Hart Crag follow the main ridge path NW then W to the summit of Fairfield.

10 DOVEDALE PATH

The shortest route from the Patterdale side but very steep with some rough terrain to cross.

Start Cow Bridge, A591 **(GR403134)**
Distance 6km (3¾ miles)
Time 2-2½ hours
Height gain 789m
Terrain woodland, steep rough valley, hanging corrie, rounded col and stony summit plateau
Difficulty strenuous
Popularity quiet

Route Follow the path SSW past Brothers Water then W up through Dovedale to gain the rough ridge that climbs SW past Dove Crag. Above Dove Crag gain the col on the SSE side of Hart Crag then follow the main ridge path as it swings W to the summit of Fairfield.

"I've climbed it"

Ann Wright, Skelmersdale

It was a cold, damp and miserable day when we decided to do Fairfield from Brothers Water. We set off through Dovedale and up to Hart Crag. We passed a guy on his way down who commented on the poor visibility on the tops, and as we approached the ridge we saw a very watery sun shining through the mist.

A few yards further on, we stepped out of the cloud and saw the most beautiful inversion over the whole of Lakeland –it looked like a giant bowl of whipped cream! After Fairfield, where the views were fantastic, we descended from Cofa Pike and were lucky enough to see a 'spectre' just at the bottom of the long haul up St Sunday Crag. In all our years we'd never seen an inversion or a spectre – it was one of those perfect days. That guy will never know what he missed (the early bird doesn't always catch the worm).

Joanne Lomas, Ripponden

Having lived in Ambleside for three years while at college, and having no transport of my own, Fairfield was the obvious choice for a 'big' mountain to climb. The first time I climbed up Nab Scar towards Fairfield, Ambleside was covered in mist with only the church spire providing any sign of the town below. Over the years the Horseshoe was completed in many different conditions, including snow, but only recently, on a return visit with my husband, was I treated to blue skies and marvellous views.

Looking forward to our first two-dayer together we climbed up to Heron Pike from Grasmere and then over Great Rigg towards Fairfield. Over lunch I was at last able to see the views I had missed so many times before.

My next challenge? To convince my husband we would be climbing St Sunday Crag before descending to Patterdale for the night.

David Sandbrook, Hook

Seven years ago I did the Fairfield Horseshoe for the first time. I went with two friends while my heavily pregnant wife explored the shops and cafés of Ambleside. It was a fantastic spring day with not a cloud in the perfect blue sky, and snow lay on the fells.

The summit of Fairfield was freezing cold and very windy so we sheltered behind rocks to eat our lunch and admire the wintry view. When we got up to set off my friend noticed the small thermometer attached to my rucksack was showing a relatively warm temperature. I had to point out that as he had been sitting on my rucksack for the last 15 minutes he was reading the temperature of his backside!

LOCATION	GALLOWAY
HEIGHT	843m/2,765ft
SUMMIT GR	NX428855

Merrick

IF YOU FEEL LIKE GETTING AWAY FROM IT ALL, HEAD FOR THE WILD OPEN SPACE OF MERRICK. IT'S THE PERFECT ANTIDOTE FOR STRESS.

Words **Jane Baker**

There are some times in life when only an empty mountain will do. One on which you can lose yourself (not literally) in endless stretches of wilderness. Solitude is the breath of fresh air that many a mountain walker seeks from time to time, and Merrick answers that call.

Leave behind the Lakes and Peaks and the hordes of trekkers. By England's standards this mountain is deserted, and the sense of freedom is liberating.

Standing proud in the Galloway Hills, this Corbett measures up as the tallest mountain in Scotland's Southern Uplands. The area has been nicknamed 'The Range of the Awful Hand', because it resembles a right hand reaching upwards. Awful, because it's a little bit crooked; but this shouldn't be taken as a literal reference to the landscape, which is rugged, wild and beautiful.

The range has five ridges, which poke up like fingers and a thumb. Guiding you in the right direction, Merrick does the job of an index finger, pointing off across vast swathes of breathtaking scenery. It has a face too. In an outcrop of rock on the south-east flank (at **NX435845**) a character known as the Grey Man of Merrick peers out in profile. Fixed in a permanent frown, there is little the light can do to soften his features, which make up one of the most famous landmarks in Galloway.

It's not just the rocky outcrops that put this mountain on the map. Fame has been heaped on these hills by literary greats, whose writings have been inspired by the surroundings. Murder Hole (**NX439829**) was immortalised in Samuel Crockett's novel *The Raiders* which was published in 1864. A scene in the book was based on the real-life murder of a peddler, whose body was dumped near a lonely junction on the road to Bargrennan. On a brighter note Sir Walter Scott expressed his profound love of the area through poetry;

Land of my sires!
What mortal hand,
Can e'er untie the filial band,
That knits me to the rugged land.

Merrick is revered by walkers and is also a spiritual home for off-road cyclists. Long before the days of full suspension, a mad-keen biker by the name of David Bell was riding his tourer all over these hills. He was a member of the Rough Tough Fellowship, a group of cycle enthusiasts who dared to take their drop handlebar bikes off the tarmac. For over 30 years he shared his adventures with the readers of the *Ayrshire Post* in a column called *The Highwayman*. Bikers can pay homage to him at a plaque on the cairn at **NX912908**.

Even dedicated walkers might want to get on two wheels to tackle this peak. Getting to the ridges from the south doesn't pose much of a problem but from the west there's a long trek through pine forests, where wheels would speed things up. The east leads in through remote heather moorland and boggy ground. Like a sponge, Merrick holds its water and on steep terrain the rock can be loose. But once you step up onto the long ridge the going gets much easier. The springy turf bowls you along as if you were walking on a mattress.

If you make the summit on a clear day the views across to Ireland, England, Scotland and the Isle of Man are spectacular. Crocket described the view from here as 'A weird wild world, new and strange, not yet out of chaos – not yet approved of by God'. It's a haven of tranquillity where land, sea and clouds merge into one with little intrusion from man.

The east is littered with lochs, which glisten like precious stones. Interestingly, Loch Enoch (near route 5) contains an island on which there is a wee loch. This may be unique in Scotland... unless readers know different!

Merrick from Snibe Hill.

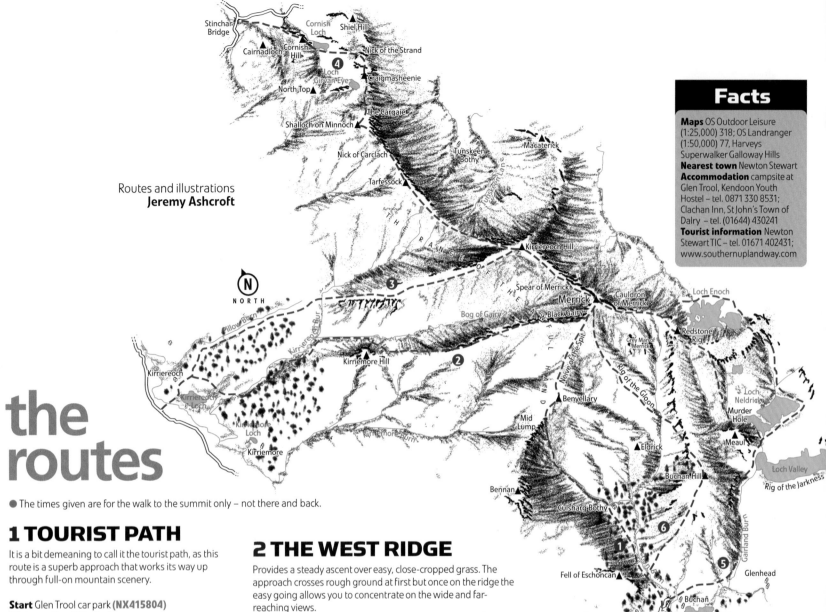

Routes and illustrations
Jeremy Ashcroft

the routes

● The times given are for the walk to the summit only – not there and back.

1 TOURIST PATH

It is a bit demeaning to call it the tourist path, as this route is a superb approach that works its way up through full-on mountain scenery.

Start Glen Trool car park (**NX415804**)
Distance 6km (3¾ miles)
Time 2½ hours
Height gain 752m
Terrain forested valley, steep corrie, grassy mountainside, narrow ridge and grassy summit plateau
Difficulty intermediate
Popularity moderate

Route From the car park follow the good path N along the burn past the Buchan Waterfall then on up the glen to Culsharg Bothy. From the bothy climb the steepening path NW then N to the shoulder on the SW side of Benyellary. Climb NE to the summit of Benyellary then head N then NE over the Neive of the Spit to the summit plateau of Merrick. Continue NE to the summit (watch out for the crags of Black Gairy which run close to the path as the summit is neared).

2 THE WEST RIDGE

Provides a steady ascent over easy, close-cropped grass. The approach crosses rough ground at first but once on the ridge the easy going allows you to concentrate on the wide and far-reaching views.

Start car park by the Water of Minnoch, Kirriereoch (**NX360866**)
Distance 8km (5 miles)
Time 2½-3 hours
Height gain 628m
Terrain forest, rough moorland, grassy rounded ridge and grassy summit plateau
Difficulty strenuous
Popularity quiet

Route Follow the track E then N then E again past Kirriereoch to a fork. Take the R branch and follow it S then E to another fork by the Kirriemore Burn. Turn R and cross the burn then follow the forest tracks E up the S side of the burn. Exit the forest and continue E alongside the burn until it is possible to climb SE up the hillside to gain the low col on the E side of Kirriemore Hill. From the col the going gets much easier. Head SE then E up the west ridge to the summit of Merrick.

3 KIRRIEREOCH HILL ROUTE

A fine high-level route that takes in the subsidiary tops of Kirriereoch Hill and the Spear of Merrick.

Start car park by the Water of Minnoch, Kirriereoch (**NX360866**)
Distance 9km (5½ miles)
Time 3 hours
Height gain 776m
Terrain forest, steep rocky ridge, high mountain ridges and grassy summits

Difficulty strenuous
Popularity quiet

Route Follow the track E then N then E again past Kirriereoch to a fork. Take the L branch and follow the track NE then E to a ridge over the Pillow Burn. Either follow the Pillow Burn E to the Cross Burn and ford it (difficult in spate) or cross the bridge and follow the track then path N then E to work through the forest to the Cross Burn and ford it (difficult in spate). Whichever way you choose you should then head SE up steepening and rough hillside above the crags to gain the west ridge of Kirriereoch Hill. Climb E up the ridge to the summit of Kirriereoch Hill. Descend SE to the col then climb steeply SE then S over the Spear of Merrick to Merrick itself.

4 THE RANGE OF THE AWFUL HAND

A tremendous route that traverses the whole length of The Range of the Awful Hand and one that should be on everyone's classic tick-list.

Start Stinchar Bridge (**NX396956**)
Distance 12km (7½ miles)
Time 4-5 hours
Height gain 1025m
Terrain forest, lochan, rough moorland, high mountain ridge, mostly grass with some rocky sections and grassy summits
Difficulty very strenuous
Popularity quiet

Route Follow the path SE through the forest to Cornish Hill. Descend slightly SE then climb Craigmasheenie. Descend S across the rough col and make the ascent above the Cargie to the Shalloch on Minnoch. This is the start of the main ridge (The Range of the Awful Hand). The crest is followed S then SSE over the Nick of Carclach, Tarfessock, Kirriereoch Hill and the Spear of Merrick to the summit of Merrick.

5 REDSTONE RIG

Explores the wild and remote lochs on Merrick's east side then makes a steep final climb up the Redstone Rig.

Start Glen Trool car park (**NX415804**)
Distance 7km (4¼ miles)
Time 2½-3 hours
Height gain 768m
Terrain forest, steep-sided glen, lochs, steep corrie, rocky hillside, rounded ridge, grassy summit
Difficulty strenuous
Popularity quiet

Route Take the track then path past the farm at Buchan to join the Gairland Burn path. Take it NE to Loch Valley then N to Loch Neldricken. Skirt N then W around the loch, then head N as the path climbs to the narrow col by Craig Neldricken. From the col turn L and head W to the foot of Redstone Rig. Climb steeply NW to the summit of Merrick.
Alternative You can skirt round the eastern shore of Loch Neldricken and climb N up the steepening corrie to gain the E side of Loch Enoch. The base of Redstone Rig is then gained by walking round the top of Loch Enoch.

6 RIG OF THE GLOON

The steep crest of the Rig of the Gloon climbs straight up the front of Merrick and can be easily combined with an ascent of the viewpoint Buchan Hill to give a short but adventurous route.

Start Glen Trool car park (**NX415804**)
Distance 2½ hours
Height gain 816m
Terrain steep rocky hill, rocky ridge, hanging corrie, steep narrow ridge and grassy summit
Difficulty strenuous
Popularity quiet

Route From the car park follow the good path N along the burn and past the Buchan Waterfall. Cross the burn and climb NE to the top of Buchan Hill. Head NNE along the crest of the Rig of Enoch. Before the head is reached descend N towards the forest edge and cross the corrie mouth NW to gain the base of the Rig of the Gloon. Climb NNW straight up its crest to gain Merrick's western shoulder. Turn R and follow the vague path NE to the top.

"I've climbed it"

C Poynter Keighley

Having turned 80 I have memories of wartime comrades, alas many long gone. However, for the past few years I have been very lucky to have a good complement of fellow walkers.

We climbed the Merrick up stony, water-filled paths onto a sodden grassy slope. The cloud descended with the drizzle and visibility deteriorated so it was a case of trying to keep in contact with the shadowy figures in front. I had visions of being lost up there forever! We went onward to the summit where the wind tried to blow our makeshift St Andrew's flag, and us, away. I felt particularly sorry for a bunch of army squaddies up there on exercise: we were out for pleasure, but they had to do it.

At Loch Enoch I slipped and fell in a burn, but I couldn't have got much wetter. The Merrick may have its share of benign days but sadly this wasn't one of them!

Keith Fergus Glasgow

It was my dad's first time climbing a Corbett and I wanted him to experience the exhilarating views and highs that I've had. Unfortunately this was not to be. At 2,000ft the conditions deteriorated into white-out and we put our faith in the compass and map. Our trust was rewarded, though, when, after 2½ hours of climbing, the trig point suddenly appeared. There was much backslapping and relief.

Our footprints were the first in the snow that day and although the views were non-existent, we felt like pioneers. There is a certain masochistic pleasure in climbing and enjoying a day on the hill in such conditions, but we did.

Andy Ritchie Darwen

My absence from this photo of the summit of Merrick is deliberate. It is to protect my identity in case my boss comes across this article! I would be in serious trouble if he found out that I had slipped away a little early from a one-day job near Ayr in order to attempt the climb.

Just as I was nearing the top a blanket of stubborn mist shrouded the summit and willingly posed for my photo. I began my descent and when I was too far away to go back the mist drifted aimlessly away.

I had bagged, but not conquered, the Merrick – so there is only one thing for it. The next time I'm working near Ayr I'll be back (but please don't tell the boss!).

LOCATION	SOUTHERN HIGHLANDS
HEIGHT	974m (3,192ft)
SUMMIT GR	NN367028

Ben Lomond

IMPRESSIVE YET ACCESSIBLE, HERE'S A MUNRO THAT'S POPULAR
WITH ALL MANNER OF MANKIND.

Words **Guy Procter**

Mallaig
Fort William
Braema
Oban
Glasgow
Edinburg

**The bonnie, bonnie
flanks of Ben Lomond.**
SCOTLAND IN FOCUS/R WEIR

71

This is the gentle Ben's dark side – much less known, sterner and harder going, a surprising look at a mountain with such a well-known public face. Think of it as the John Leslie route.

Like Sean Connery or Lulu, Ben Lomond is for many a Sassenach the acceptable face of Scotland. Neither too hard-faced nor unapproachable, the ageless good looks of the most southerly Munro are the perfect PR face for Mountainous Scotland.

It's the first really impressive peak you see on the drive up from Glasgow, and for that reason alone it becomes for many their first Munro. Yes, it's one of those mountains that attracts the whole spectrum of walkers – from the carrier bag and pushchair crowd to hoary old baggers. But don't get the impression that it's a soft touch; the pull up from Rowardennan is a protracted wrestle with gravity from which anyone emerging victorious deserves credit.

It's not technically difficult – there are no narrow arêtes to turn the vertiginous stomach, or will-I-be-able-to-get-down-this-again scrambles – but it is a sweat. The going will be familiar to anyone who has walked the Lakeland fells, but in common with many other Scottish hills there's a prologue of woodland walking. Once you clear the trees, those who like to know the worst will be delighted to find they can see the whole way to the summit almost right away.

Unlike some mountains though, Ben Lomond's straightforwardness doesn't make it bland. Being a monstrous peak islanded in a relatively flat landscape gives it on-tiptoe views in all directions. It's a good reason to keep stopping as you stump ever (and sometimes it will feel like forever) upwards.

It's a long, steady drag from the start at Rowardennan, but the last hundred feet before the summit gather sharply in steepness and give the summit a particularly good angle on the loch below and the peaks to the west – salty characters like The Cobbler and Beinn Narnain.

People will never be impressed by your climbing a mountain unless it's the sort you could fall off, and you'll be pleased to hear that with Ben Lomond you could, just. You'd really have to be trying though – the path is very well-walked and difficult to stray from all the way to the boxing-ring-sized summit.

For the same impress-your-neighbours reasons, you can't help but wish the name Ben Lomond meant something like 'Cruel Peak' or 'The Devil's Icebucket'. But sadly it actually translates as 'Beacon Hill' – which makes it sound uncomfortably like somewhere near Guildford which may or may not have supported a fire up a stick at one time or another. Best keep that under your hat.

One facet of Ben Lomond does gleam though – the stones which bejewel the path near the top. They're rich in some (to me) unknown mineral which lends them a creamy metallic lustre in bright sunshine. If you rub them some of it comes off on your fingers like you've been helping a toddler make Christmas cards.

Dedicated anti-socialists or people who've already climbed the Rowardennan path can choose the ascent from the mountain's eastern side. The track, from the B829 at Loch Dhu, leads you into the altogether lonelier and steeper auditorium of the eastern corrie. This is the gentle Ben's dark side – much less known, sterner and harder going, a surprising look at a mountain with such a well-known public face. Think of it as the John Leslie route.

Unlike in the Lake District where the hills are packed in like a well-stocked fruitbowl and you can gorge on three or more in a day, in Scotland that's a rare treat. Here the scale is bigger – the peaks are more numerous but more widely scattered; Ben Lomond is very definitely a meal to itself. Don't expect to get much change out of a day, but don't resign yourself to an up-and-back walk either. The ridge to the west of the summit leads to the unkempt outlier, Ptarmigan, from where you can complete a circular route by heading south back down to the forested fringe of the loch.

Ben Lomond bears the same relation to the rest of the Highlands as Orrest Head does to the Lake District. It was that hill – a magnificent viewpoint and a bridge between the familiar world to the south and a new one to the north – which ignited the young Wainwright's passion for the fells. If Scotland is something of an unknown continent to you, there's no better place to start exploring it than this.

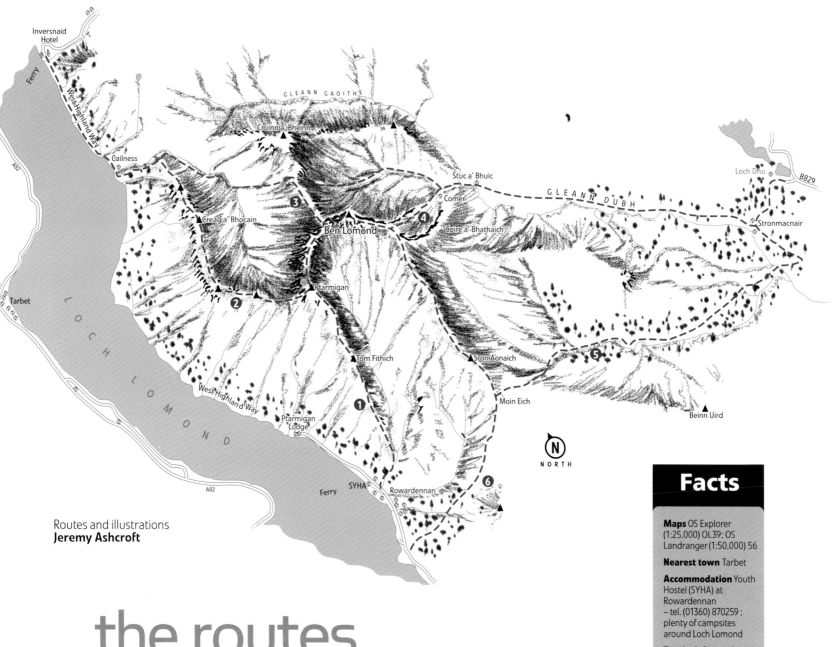

Routes and illustrations
Jeremy Ashcroft

the routes

● The times given are for the walk to the summit only – not there and back.

1 PTARMIGAN RIDGE

The Ptarmigan Ridge takes you along the western arm of Ben Lomond's southern corrie and this high-level narrow ridge makes a superb route either in ascent or descent. Check it out!

Start Rowardennan **(NS360994)**
Distance 5km (3 miles)
Time 2½ hours
Height gain 967m

Terrain steep hillside, steep ridge, exposed col and steep rocky ridge
Difficulty strenuous
Popularity moderate
Route From the minor road N of Rowardennan take the path that climbs steeply N to Tom Fithich. Pass Tom Fithich and continue north up the steepening ridge to the summit of Ptarmigan. Follow the crest of the undulating ridge N then NE to the col at the base of the NW ridge. Follow this to the summit of Ben Lomond.

Facts

Maps OS Explorer (1:25,000) OL39; OS Landranger (1:50,000) 56

Nearest town Tarbet

Accommodation Youth Hostel (SYHA) at Rowardennan – tel. (01360) 870259 ; plenty of campsites around Loch Lomond

Tourist information Tarbet – tel. (01301) 702260

Best pub Inversnaid Hotel – tel. (01877) 386223

2 CREAG A' BHOCAIN RIDGE

This route provides you with a long, airy approach to Ptarmigan over the minor summits of Creag a' Bhochain. Situated high above the waters of Loch Lomond, the views up and down the loch are stunning.

Start Inversnaid Hotel (**NN338088**)
Distance 9km (5½ miles)
Time 3½ hours
Height gain 1044m
Terrain woodland, steep hillside, undulating ridge, broad col, exposed col and steep rocky ridge
Difficulty strenuous
Popularity quiet
Route Cross the bridge and head S along the West Highland Way to Cailness. Climb the steep hillside on the S side of Cailness Burn then turn S and traverse the numerous little peaks of Creag a' Bhochain to the broad col below the W slopes of Ptarmigan. Head E and work your way up steep ground to the crest of the Ptarmigan. Once on the ridge follow it NE to the col at the base of the NW ridge. Follow the ridge to the summit of Ben Lomond.

3 NORTH RIDGE

Ben Lomond's great north ridge provides a natural and very attractive route. Its crest is grassy and easy to follow, and it can be gained either from Cailness on the Loch Lomond side or from the Gleann Dubh side.

Start B829 near Loch Dhu (**NN434037**)
Distance 11km (6¾ miles)
Time 3½-4 hours
Height gain 921m
Terrain woodland, long glen, steep-sided corrie, broad col, steep mountain ridge and steep rocky ridge
Difficulty strenuous
Popularity quiet
Route Follow the forest track around Loch Dhu then S over the low ridge to Stronmacnair. At the junction turn R and follow the track NW up Gleann Dubh past Stùc a' Bhuic to the bridge across the Abhainn Gaoith. Cross the bridge and follow the Caorainn Achaidh Burn NW then SW until it is possible to climb the back wall of the corrie to the col on the S side of Cruinn a' Bheinn. From the col, climb the crest of the N ridge to the col at the base of the NW ridge, and follow this to the summit of Ben Lomond.
Variation You can reach the col at the base of the N ridge from the Loch Lomond side by climbing
E then SE on the S side of Cailness Burn.

4 NORTH-EAST RIDGE

This route first climbs the SE crest of Ben Lomond's north-facing summit corrie. It is remote and very lonely, but this side of Ben Lomond is especially worth exploring in winter when the corrie can provide some excellent short winter climbs.

Start B829 near Loch Dhu (**NN434037**)

Distance 9.5km (6 miles)
Time 3½ hours
Height gain 921m
Terrain woodland, long glen, steep-sided corrie and steep rocky ridge
Difficulty strenuous
Popularity quiet

Route Follow the forest track around Loch Dhu then S over the low ridge to Stronmacnair. At the junction turn R and follow the track NW up Gleann Dubh past Stùc a' Bhuic to the farm at Comer. Climb steeply SW alongside the burn until it enters the corrie on the N side of Ben Lomond. Climb the crest of the ridge SE to join the main summit ridge which you follow NW to the summit rocks.

5 BRUACH CAORAINN BURN ROUTE

This route gives you a long eastern approach to the Tourist Route.

Start B829 near Loch Dhu (**NN434037**)
Distance 13km (8 miles)
Time 3½-4 hours
Height gain 921m
Terrain woodland, long glen, broad open col, rounded mountain ridge and rocky summit ridge
Difficulty easy
Popularity moderate
Route Follow the forest track around Loch Dhu then S over the low ridge to Stronmacnair. At the junction turn L and follow the track SE down Gleann Dubh for nearly one mile to another junction. Turn R and follow the track then path west, alongside Bruach Caorainn Burn to the broad open col of Moin Eich. Continue W over the col to join the path which climbs N then NW to the summit of Ben Lomond.

6 TOURIST ROUTE

This is the one that your Uncle Alf and Aunty Maude have probably tackled, so combine it with something else for good measure. It's the main route up Ben Lomond and being so close to Glasgow it is very popular. Most of the way it is a constructed path which means it's easy to follow. But under a covering of snow and with the cloud down many have discovered the sting in the tail of this seemingly easy plod.

Start car park at Rowardennan (**NS360987**)
Distance 6km (3¾ miles)
Time 2 hours
Height gain 952m
Terrain woodland, steep hillside, rounded mountain ridge and rocky summit ridge
Difficulty easy
Popularity very busy
Route From the car park follow the broad path NE through the woodland then N up the rounded south ridge of Ben Lomond. As you reach the summit ridge the ground steepens a little and the path turns NW to gain the summit rocks.

"I've climbed it"

Brian Brown Kilmartin

My aim to climb all of the Munros is one of the very long-term variety. Sometimes things like having sons and daughters gets in the way.

So, a walk up the tourist drag of Ben Lomond on December 29 1992 was the first for a couple of years. What transpired was one of my best mountain days anywhere, anytime.

Leaving home in darkness, Bill and I arrived at Rowardennan at first light, a freezing cold morning under a layer of grey cloud. We left the car park following the main path on what was a bit of a slog after such a long lay-off.

As we got higher the cloud thinned and glimpses of sunshine gave us hope we would eventually come out above the cloud. Sure enough as we climbed and the cloud level sank we emerged at about 2,000ft to glorious blue skies and bright sun. All around, hilltops peeked through the cloud like little islands in a sea of white cloud.

The ground was hard and icy but not difficult, and the walk up to the summit was pure pleasure. It was a bit too cold to stop for long; we nevertheless enjoyed some hot soup and sarnies before taking loads of photographs and descending.

A great day – a day when just being on the mountain was a privilege.

Stewart Fairhurst
Merseyside

As we climbed through the woodlands and over the 'Granny Stopper' – an awkwardly shaped rock which requires a careful step or two – we emerged out into the open, following a well-defined path leading to the summit.

Ben Lomond stood proud, almost beckoning us onwards with a smile as if to say 'not much further now!'

Just before the top, along came the rain hand in hand with its friend the mist; but this did not deter us. We soon stood on the summit, filled with a sense of achievement and honoured just to be there. This Munro had presented us with a demanding climb to its summit and gave us memories that we all can cherish for quite some time to come... which was exactly what we did over that first pint in the pub when we'd made it back down!

LOCATION	NW HIGHLANDS
HEIGHT	1062m (3,483ft)
SUMMIT GR	NH 069834 (BIDEIN A' GHLAS THUILL)

An Teallach

CLIMB THE 'STEGOSAURUS' OF THE HIGHLANDS, WHERE ANCIENT CLAN FEUDS ONCE RESULTED IN MURDERS MOST FOUL...

Words **Piers Pickard** Photography **Tom Bailey**

An Teallach is larger than life in every way. Its history is full of murder most foul. Its size, beauty and fearsome reputation elevate it to the status of Supermunro. Take the mass, the sheer bulk of Ben Nevis, cross it with the steep, airy spikiness of the Cuillin, and you get An Teallach. It's the stegosaurus of the Scottish hills.

To do a full traverse of the mountain requires a long, long day out. If you stay strictly to the ridge proper (there is an easier path), you'll be rock-climbing at Diff grade. In winter conditions, it's a Grade 2-3 epic that ranks as one of Britain's finest alpine routes. John MacCulloch tried it in 1824 and thought it would never end: "I continued along the giddy ridge, in the hope of seeing its termination; but all continued vacant, desolate, silent, dazzling and boundless... its apparent altitude greater than any single mountain in Scotland, excepting perhaps Ben Nevis."

It stands as the northern sentinel of the area known as 'The Great Wilderness'. This area lives up to its name, containing Scotland's most remote Munro, Á Mhaighdean, which lies a blister-popping 21km from the road at Poolewe.

But it's not just the scenery that's larger than life; the history of the region is, too. For this is the scene of the brutal murder of Scotland's very own Romeo....

Ullapool

Inverness

llaig

"Allan's head was flung into a stream"

In the 15th century all the Gairloch region, including An Teallach, was MacLeod country. They were a jealous clan, proud of their blood and family name, and hateful of the other Highland clans. And the family they hated most were the MacKenzies.

Then, in the 1470s, along came one Allan MacLeod, the Highlands' 'Oor Romeo', who gave his heart to a MacKenzie girl. His Juliet wasn't just any MacKenzie; she was the daughter of Alexander the Upright, sixth Laird of Kintail and sworn enemy to the MacLeods. In spite of fierce opposition, Allan married the girl he adored, hoping it would draw their clans closer and end the bad blood between them.

For a few years they lived happily on a little island in Loch Tollaidh. Allan's wife bore him two little boys, who were his pride and joy. Sadly this blissful existence was not to last. One fine and sunny day, Allan rowed across the loch to go fishing on the River Ewe. It was a hot day, the fish weren't biting, and he soon found himself streched out in the sun, snoring happily.

Allan's two brothers (who lived on Lewis) resented the fact that their wayward brother had sullied the MacLeod lineage by producing heirs that were half-MacKenzie. They saw Allan's boat at the edge of the loch and guessed where he was. Together they crept up on their sleeping kinsman and murdered him where he lay, flinging his severed head down into a stream where it was carried off by the current...

The ruthless killers rowed back across the lake, stormed into Allan's house and found his two sons playing beside their mother. They snatched the two small boys and cheerfully told Allan's wife exactly what they'd done to her beloved husband. They didn't bother to kill her, but left the distraught woman wailing and crying. She tried to follow them to save her sons, and eventually ran into an old servant of her husband. She persuaded the man to find the brothers and see what could be done. He crept up to the murderers' camp, but what he saw made his blood run cold. There, suspended from a tree were two little shirts covered in blood, hanging up as trophies. It was too late, the boys were already dead.

The grief-stricken woman returned to her father, Alexander the Upright, and told him what had happened. The tale was so horrific, he would not believe it until she produced the blood-caked shirts as proof. Alexander immediately dispatched his son to Edinburgh with the shirts, to show the King. James III was rightly horrified, and gave the MacKenzies the go-ahead to wreak a savage revenge: "a commission of fire and sword for the destruction of the MacLeods".

So today, as you stand on the summit of mighty An Teallach and look west towards Gairloch, you can see the landscape won by the Upright MacKenzies with the King's blessing. Love might not always conquer all, but the view certainly takes some beating!

The brooding black waters of Loch Toll an Lochain nestle below Bidean a' Ghlas Thuill.

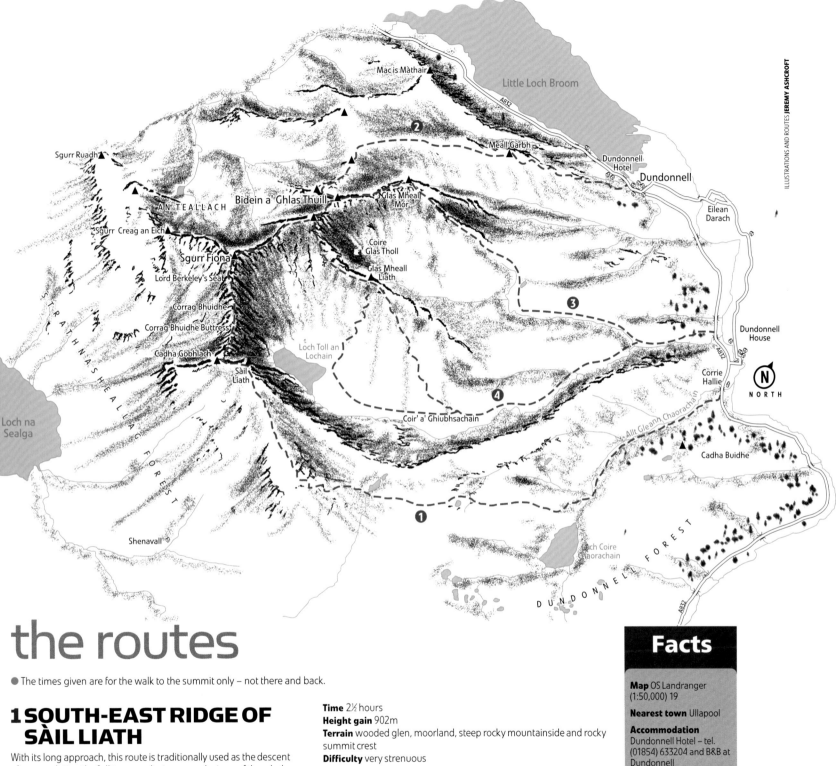

the routes

● The times given are for the walk to the summit only – not there and back.

1 SOUTH-EAST RIDGE OF SÀIL LIATH

With its long approach, this route is traditionally used as the descent after completing the full traverse. It gives superb views of the whole ridge and for the most part covers distance at an easy gradient. The last part, up the shoulder of Sàil Liath, is steep but it's not without interest as there are plenty of rocks to scramble over.

Start Corrie Hallie **(NH114850)**
Distance 6.2km (3¾ miles)

Time 2½ hours
Height gain 902m
Terrain wooded glen, moorland, steep rocky mountainside and rocky summit crest
Difficulty very strenuous
Popularity quiet

Route From the road at Corrie Hallie take the access track SW as it climbs on the S side of the Allt Gleann Chaorchain onto open moorland and the junction with the Shenavall path. Turn R and follow the path SW for about 1km after which you can leave it and make the steepening ascent W then NW to the summit of Sàil Liath.

Facts

Map OS Landranger (1:50,000) 19

Nearest town Ullapool

Accommodation Dundonnell Hotel – tel. (01854) 633204 and B&B at Dundonnell

Tourist information – tel. (01854) 612135

2 THE MEALL GARBH ROUTE

A well-graded path which climbs in manageable steps first up Meall Garbh then past Glas Mheall Mòr to make a short pull to Bidein a' Ghlas Thuill. This is probably the most popular approach to start the traverse as it means you can abseil down the climbing pitch; however it can also be recommended for the descent as it's easier on tired legs and hits the road near Dundonnell Hotel.

Start Dundonnell (**NH093878**)
Distance 6km (3¾ miles)
Time 2½ hours
Height gain 1052m
Terrain steep craggy mountainside, rounded spur, broad ridge, exposed col and rocky summit crest
Difficulty very strenuous
Popularity quiet

Route From the road follow the path as it zig-zags S then WSW up the crest of Meall Garbh to the broad col on the main ridge. Climb S, SW then SE to the unnamed top on the W side of Glas Mheall Mór. Descend S to the exposed col, then climb steeply S up the narrow crest to the summit of Bidein a' Ghlas Thuill.

3 GLAS MHEALL MÓR ROUTE

Direct ascent which takes in Glas Mheall Mór and has the advantage of shortening the road work if you are doing the complete traverse; however, the final section is a real thigh-buster.

Start A832, N of Corrie Hallie (**NH862857**)
Distance 4km (2½ miles)
Time 2½ hours
Height gain 1128m

An Teallach's exposed ridges rise up in rocky sections, making it look like a knobbly-backed stegosaurus.

Terrain wooded glen, steep corrie, very steep scree-strewn slopes and rocky summit crest
Difficulty very strenuous
Popularity quiet

Route From the road follow the N side of the burn that drains Coire a' Ghlas Thuill WSW to the mouth of the corrie, then turn NW and follow a zigzagging ascent up the very steep slopes to the summit of Glas Mheall Mór. Head SW down the crest of the ridge and over the col to the unnamed top. Turn S and descend to the exposed col, cross it, then climb steeply S up the narrow crest to summit of Bidein a' Ghlas Thuill.

4 GLAS MHEALL LIATH ROUTE

Just as impressive as the sandstone pinnacles of the main ridge is the massively proportioned corrie of Toll an Lochain. Combine a visit with an ascent of Glas Meall Liath to provide arguably the best route onto the main ridge.

Start A832, N of Corrie Hallie (**NH862857**)
Distance 5km (3 miles)
Time 2½ hours
Height gain 1050m
Terrain wooded glen, steep corrie, very steep scree-strewn slopes and rocky summit crest
Difficulty very strenuous
Popularity quiet

Route From the road follow the N side of the burn SW into the Coir' a' Ghiubhsachain then W up into Toll an Lochain. You can make the steep ascent to Glas Mheall Liath either from the head of Coir' a' Ghiubhsachain by zigzagging NW or you can do it from the mouth of the loch by zigzagging N. From the summit of Glas Mheall Liath climb W along the crest to Bidein a' Ghlas Thuill.

THE TRAVERSE

Making a crossing of the spectacular sandstone pinnacles which form the ridge between Sàil Liath to the south and Bidein a' Ghlas Thuill to the north constitutes one of the best British scrambles. Route-finding is simple: either you follow the crest which goes at mostly Grade 2/3 with one pitch of climbing at Difficult (under snow and ice it's a Winter 2/3), or you take the exposed but easier path on the western side of the crest which skirts the hardest bits but still warrants a scrambling Grade 2/3. The routes described previously only detail ascents of Sàil Liath and Bidein a' Ghlas Thuill; if you intend to complete the full traverse you will need to add at least another 7 hours.

"I've climbed it"

Bob Clare Preston

Sgurr Fiona was my first Munro, climbed in September 1996, with my friend Geoff. The day dawned bright and clear but as we set off from Corrie Hallie car park, the sun disappeared beneath a vast canopy of cloud. As we scaled Sàil Liath we were overtaken by four youths from Leicester who bounded up behind us. On the other side, we met a couple from Stockport, Tony and Liz. They were somewhat disorientated by the mist and latched onto us and the Leicester boys. So there we were, all eight of us finding our way around by committee. Tony and Liz lost their map in a sudden gust so I lent them my spare, while the lads headed off to climb the Pinnacles. They disappeared into the mist – in the wrong direction – and returned minutes later. Geoff and I weren't interested in the Pinnacles, so pressed on for the main summit. We headed into the mist on a side path, only to find we'd gone the wrong way too!

After lunch we headed up to Sgurr Fiona, our bearings confirmed by the presence of the Gang of Four (who had already traversed the Pinnacles), Liz and Tony.

Although Tony's mountain skills had seemed wanting earlier, he proved much more expert than we'd guessed. He led us down the tricky arête between Sgurr Fiona and Bidein, and up to Bidein itself. From here he located a gully which gave us a direct route back to Corrie Hallie. We passed through a stupendous corrie – tantalisingly revealed by a break in the cloud. Far below we saw the four boys for the last time, charging across the heather.

Barry Arblaster Chesterfield

I decided to climb An Teallach when I read that more people had died on it than on any other mountain in Scotland. Although morbid, the idea appealed to my sense of adventure!

The day came and my brother and I set off from the car park, glancing up at the craggy summit with nervous apprehension. My fears proved well-founded when, after a strenuous walk, I finally reached the Corrag Bhuidhe Buttress – a ridge of smooth rock with steep drops on all sides. Friction was the only thing keeping me from falling!

My hands began slipping and fierce winds were scaring me silly. I succumbed to full-blown vertigo and had to return to the base of the ridge and take the bypass path up, instead. My legs and hands were shaking until we were safely past the ridge and standing on Sgurr Fiona's summit.

Buachaille Etive Mór

Tune in for the lowdown on a mountain that strikes a chord with walkers and climbers alike.

WORDS BEN WINSTON

f mountains were musical instruments, then Buachaille Etive Mór would be a trumpet. Not because of its appearance (conical) or because it's in a band (Scottish, rock) but because it heralds your arrival at Glen Coe. It looms with a great fanfare after the bleak wastes of Rannoch Moor, greeting you with the fearsome Stob Dearg, one of the most instantly recognisable peaks in the UK.

Stob Dearg, or Red Peak, is one of two Munros that make up the Buachaille (or 'the Buckle' if you're in the know). The other, stretched out at the far end of a long and impressive ridge, is Stob na Bròige, which translates, rather curiously, as 'Peak of the Shoe'. Together with the tops of Stob na Doire and Stob Coire Altruim, these make up the long stretch of mountain that earns the full title Buachaille Etive Mór (which, for those into translation, means 'The Big Shepherd of Etive).

The Big Shepherd basks in the dawn sunshine.

Facts

Maps OS Outdoor Leisure (1:25,000) 38; OS Landranger (1:50,000) 41; Harveys Superwalker (1:25,000) Glen Coe; Harveys Walker (1:40,000) Glen Coe

Nearest town
Fort William

Accommodation
Youth Hostel – tel. (01855) 811219; hotel and bunkhouse: Kings House Hotel – tel. (01855) 851259; hotels, B&B and campsites in Glencoe

Tourist information
Ballachulish – tel. (01855) 811296

But there are plenty more names to this mountain. Since the days when nailed boots were popular and stiff, woolly jackets were, well, trendy, the Buachaille has been drawing climbers and mountaineers to its awesome faces. Reputations have been forged here. Norman Collie, creator of the first neon lamp and distinguished Victorian chemist, gave the world the Buachaille's first recorded route: Collie's Climb. Then Harold Raeburn put up Crowberry Gully in winter. Better still, the already-famous Abraham brothers added to their reputation with the all-time classic climb of Crowberry Ridge. And that's just the start. Now the huge cliffs of solid rhyolite that peel down from the summit of Stob Dearg hold other routes whose names inspire fear, trepidation or just a profound sense of history, of which Curved Ridge (Grade 3 scramble), the Shibboleth (E2 climb), Raven's Gully (summer HVS or winter Grade V) and the Chasm (summer VS or winter Grade V) are just a few.

So where in this great directory of antiquity and mountainous achievement do we find space for the walker? Simple – the entire ridge of the Buachaille is one of Glen Coe's classic routes. It takes you up to the summit of Stob Dearg through the surprisingly amenable Coire na Tulaich, just west of the impenetrable climbers' playground. It then leads you on a 2½ mile traverse above Glen Etive, staying high and revelling in its position at the head of the two glens, commanding views over the Aonach Eagach to Ben Nevis, down to shapely Ben Starav, over to Black Mount and across the apparently endless miles of Rannoch Moor.

But be warned: for all the Shepherd's undoubted appeal, this can be a dangerous mountain. Coire na Tulaich is a notorious avalanche blackspot in heavy snows, and the cliffs of Stob Dearg are unforgiving. But if you treat it with respect and in poor visibility follow the secret code from the summit cairn (253 degrees for 250 metres, then 280 degrees for 400 metres), you will add your name to the many thousands of walkers and climbers to whom Buachaille Etive Mór means not just 'keeper of sheep' and 'holder of a hallowed place in mountaineering history', but also 'a very special place' and 'a truly great hill'. Enjoy.

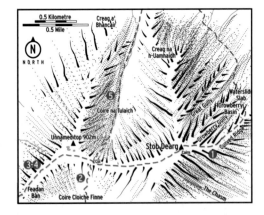

ILLUSTRATIONS AND ROUTES JEREMY ASHCROFT

Boys just wanna have fun! Curved Ridge provides one of Scotland's best scrambles – as top mountaineer Alan Hinkes will no doubt testify.

TOM BAILEY

Routes

● The times given are for the walk to the summit only – not there and back.

1 CURVED RIDGE

Curved Ridge climbs from Crowberry Basin to the top of Crowberry Tower. It passes through the magnificent rock scenery of Stob Dearg's north-east face – providing one of Scotland's best scrambles.

Start Altnafeadh, **GR221563**
Distance 1¾ miles (2.8km)
Time 3½ hours
Height gain 732m
Terrain steep mountainside, steep rocky arête and rocky summit
Difficulty strenuous (Grade 2/3 scramble, Grade 2/3 winter climb)
Popularity moderate

Route Cross the footbridge and follow the path S to a Y junction. Take the L fork and follow the path SE to the Waterslide Slab then make the steep zigzag approach up into Crowberry Basin. Head to the L of Crowberry Basin to gain the base of Curved Ridge which is the furthest L of the ridges. Climb the crest of the Curved Ridge to the cairn below Crowberry Tower. From the cairn traverse L then ascend the final rocks to the summit of Stob Dearg.

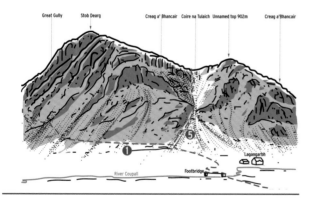

Above: choose your route! Right: the sunny side of the Buckle.

2 COIRE CLOICHE FINNE

Climbs steeply north from Glen Etive via Coire Cloiche Finne to join the main ridge of Buachaille Etive Mór on the west side of Stob Dearg. To reach the main summit, follow the steep, rocky ridge east to the summit cairn. A good alternative route if Coire na Tulaich is excessively icy or avalanche-prone.

Start Glen Etive **GR219520**
Distance 2 miles (3.2km)
Time 2½ hours
Height gain 834m
Terrain steep-sided glen, hanging corrie, scree, high mountain ridges and rocky summit
Difficulty strenuous
Popularity quiet
Variation Can also be started from Lagangarbh by following the path up to the Waterslide then traversing under the crags of Stob Dearg to the mouth of Coire Cloiche Finne.

Route From Glen Etive climb steeply N through Coire Cloiche Finne to gain the col on the SW side of Stob Dearg. From the col turn R and climb NE up the crest of the rocky ridge to the summit of Stob Dearg.

3 SRON AN FHORSAIR

A rewarding route climbing steeply south-east from Dalness onto the main ridge, which it then traverses, finishing on the main summit, Stob Dearg.

Start Glen Etive **GR185511**
Distance 4 miles (6.4 km)
Time 4 hours
Height gain (1268m)
Terrain steep ridge, high mountain ridge and rocky summit
Difficulty strenuous
Popularity quiet

Route From the roadside in Glen Etive climb Sròn an Fhorsair NW to its top at the SW end of the main Buachaille Etive Mór ridge. From the minor top follow the crest of the ridge over Stob na Bròige, Stob na Doire and Feadan Bàn to the summit of Stob Dearg.

4 COIRE ALTRUIM

Provides a straightforward route onto the main ridge from the Lairig Gartain. The easiest route off the main ridge.

Start A82, Glen Coe **GR213560**
Distance 4¼ miles (6.8km)
Time 3 hours
Height gain 871m
Terrain steep-sided glen, high corrie, high mountain ridge and rocky summit
Difficulty intermediate
Popularity quiet
Variation can also be started from Dalness **(GR171514)** by taking the Lairig Gartain path to the foot of Coire Altruim

Route From the A82 follow the Lairig Gartain SW down the glen for 2.5km. Leave the path and climb steeply SSE alongside the Allt Coire Altruim into Coire Altruim. Continue SSE and climb the coire head wall to gain the main ridge at the col on the SW side of Stob na Doire.

From the col follow the crest of the ridge NE over Stob na Doire and Feadan Bàn to the summit of Stob Dearg.

5 COIRE NA TULAICH PATH (LAGANGARBH COIRE)

The most popular 'up and down' route and one that should not be underestimated.
The head wall of the corrie is steep; it can be problematic when icy and suicidal in avalanche conditions. Climbs directly south from Lagangarbh to the col on the west side of Stob Dearg.

Start Altnafeadh, **GR221563**

Distance 2 miles (3.2km)
Time 2–2½ hours
Height gain 743m
Terrain steep rocky corrie, steep head wall, high mountain ridge and rocky summit.
Difficulty intermediate (under snow cover the corrie head wall becomes very steep)
Popularity busy

Route Cross the footbridge and follow the path S to a Y junction. Take the R fork and climb S then SSW up through the narrow confines of Coire na Tulaich. As the corrie steepens into the head wall continue SSE and make the final climb to the col on the SW side of Stob Dearg. From the col turn L and climb NE up crest of the rocky ridge to the summit of Stob Dearg.

All along the plateau of Buachaille Etive Mór, Creise and Meall a' Bhuiridh rising from the River Etive.

All quiet on Stob na Doire.

On the way down Coire na Tulaich.

"I've climbed it"

Martin Brooker,
Manchester

In August 1977 I clumsily shattered my leg playing football. The injury was severe and I was told I would be permanently disabled and would walk with a limp. What news! After three operations and several weeks in hospital I was lying at home with metalwork in the leg when my buddy Steve came round and promised, nay vowed, we'd one day do all the biggest hills in the UK, even if he had to drag me up.

In September 1999 the big trip to Scotland was planned. On the final day we climbed Buachaille Etive Mór in perfect weather – I'm sure I saw a golden eagle and deer near the top. A great, long day, some unplanned scrambling and high-level walking that will take some beating. The sheer elation of looking down on the A82 was something that will stay with me forever. It topped a great week and proved I still had a leg capable of dragging me up places. What do doctors know?!

By the time we slithered back down my scars were red raw and blistering but I had the biggest, cheesiest grin seen in Glen Coe for a long time. We may not have done the Cuillin, but it's on the list.

Mark Tagholm, London

As my friend and I drank coffee in the lounge of the Kings House Hotel, people kept coming in and greeting each other warmly – smiles, handshakes, hugs. After quarter of an hour they left but, as we were toiling up Coire Na Tulaich, we caught sight of them again. But this time they had balloons attached to their rucksacks! Was this some new elevation device from Berghaus? For the full length of the Buachaille, from Stob Dearg to Stob na Bròige, we followed these balloons, bobbing like fishermen's floats against the backdrop of Glen Coe's mountains. Finally we caught up with this seemingly eccentric group as they were supping champagne from plastic cups. I enquired what the party was for and a woman, pointing to a man leaning against the cairn, told us he had just completed his last Munro. Approaching him, I held out my hand and offered hearty congratulations. Good man! Great mountain!

ASHLEY COOPER

LOCATION	**WESTERN HIGHLANDS**
HEIGHT	**1068m (3,504ft)**
SUMMIT GR	**978168**

Sgurr Fhuaran
(Five Sisters of Kintail)

Loitering gracefully on the skyline above Glen Shiel, the Five Sisters form
one of the most enchanting ridges in Scotland. Pure Highland magic.

BOB ATKINS

The Five Sisters with Sgurr Fhuaran rising to dominance in the middle.

Facts

Maps OS Outdoor Leisure (1:25,000) 5 & 7, OS Landranger (1:50,000) 33, Harveys Superwalker (1:25,000) Kintail
Nearest town
Shiel Bridge
Accommodation
B&Bs, hotel and campsites at Shiel Bridge. SYHA Hostels at Ratagan and Alltbeith
Tourist information
Kyle of Lochalsh – tel. (01599) 534276

While everything in this world has a story, there are some things that cannot be explained by a single tale alone, and so rely on many. The Five Sisters of Kintail are one of these although they remain best introduced with the original legend, which runs something like this...

Once upon a time an Irish soldier fell for the youngest of five beautiful sisters who lived on a farm. As protocol dictated she could not marry before her siblings, the suitor was despatched to collect his four brothers and bring them back for marriage. He departed and slowly the weeks of waiting turned into months, then years, and the sisters began to worry about their age and youthful looks. Eventually, desperate not to lose their charms, they went to the local witch who turned them into the mountain range we see today, thereby proving beauty is timeless and that men are indeed all bastards. But rumour has it that if someone from the right Irish lineage returns to these mountains and kisses them then the five sisters will reappear, bright, fresh, young and ready for a wedding.

Another story says there were seven sisters to begin with, and two shipwrecked Irish princes...

And yet another mentions a wizard...

An entirely more prosaic approach to understanding the Five Sisters says they are composed of rock belonging to the Moine supergroup, which is 1,000 million years old and features psammitic granulite, quartz mica schist and mica schist. This tale includes intense heat and pressure of its own kind (geological) and features a profound geological break (the Sgurr Beag slide), but lacks any sense of the fabulous.

What is for certain is that as the present draws closer, the sisters' history becomes less ambiguous and prone to flights of fancy. It is therefore recorded as solid fact that the late, great Percy Unna, one-time president of the Scottish Mountaineering Club, bought the land and gave it to the National Trust for safekeeping. It is also fact that it takes 10 miles and over 1500 metres of ascent to get to know the Sisters properly. Further truths tell us the ascent to Sgurr na Ciste Duibhe is the longest 40 degree slope in Scotland (1000m), and the seductive skyline is one of the country's most photographed. Equally true is that the Sisters don't allow stalking on their flanks and on a fine day you can see Skye, Glen Affric and Ben Nevis from their summits. Otters and golden eagles are also relatively common.

But facts are inevitably limited in their power to express and, just as in the days after the Sisters first appeared, the way to really appreciate their charms is to walk

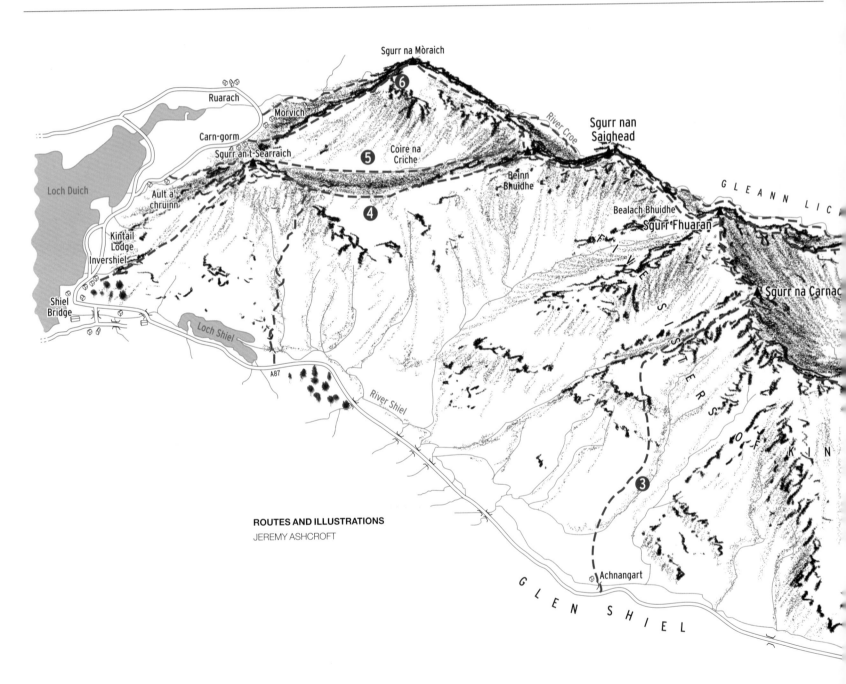

ROUTES AND ILLUSTRATIONS
JEREMY ASHCROFT

with them. Only then can you listen to their true story, hearing with your footsteps either sorry disappointment or immortality's joy. You can share your lunch at their table and explore the playground of their rocky scrambles. You can enjoy their timeless Highland view. But remember that although an accommodating bunch, the Sisters are strong-headed and march east to west decisively. If you meet one, make sure you're free to meet them all.

Unless you are a puckering Irish prince, of course. Or even an Irishman of uncertain lineage. While still welcome, you'll have to promise to keep to your feet and not at any point plant your lips to the ground. Smitten you may be (as many are), but your kiss would be the robbery of a nation. Although it would end a fable quite nicely...

From Sgurr Fhuaran, Sgurr nan Saighead and Beinn Bhuidhe lead into the distance.

PAUL MILLIGAN

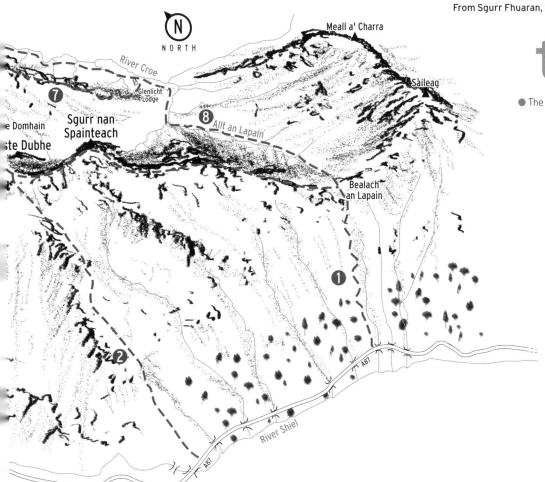

the routes

● The times given are for the walk to the summit only – not there and back.

1 BEALACH AN LAPAIN ROUTE

The full traverse of the Five Sisters is best done from east to west as the views out to sea are superb – regarded by many as the best in the north-west Highlands – and the ascent via Bealach an Lapain is better graded and an easier route than from the Shiel Bridge end.

Start A87, Glen Shiel **(GR007136)**
Distance 6km (3¾ miles)
Time 3-4 hours
Height gain 1187m
Terrain steep-sided glen, steep mountainside, exposed col, narrow rocky ridge and steep summit cone
Difficulty strenuous
Popularity moderate

Route From the road climb steeply N up the hillside at the gap between the two forestry plantations to the Bealach an Lapain. From the col make the steady climb W along the crest of the main ridge over Sgurr nan Spainteach (named after defeated Spanish soldiers fleeing from the battle of Glenshiel) to the first of the Five Sisters – Sgurr na Ciste Duibhe. Descend W then NW down the main ridge to a col at the head of Coire Domhain. From the col the ridge turns N and you follow it over Sgurr na Carnach (sister number two) to Sgurr Fhuaran (sister number three).

93

The Sisters turn their faces to the sun.

2 SOUTH FLANK OF SGURR NA CISTE DUIBHE

A direct ascent of one of the longest slopes in the Highlands. As you slog your way up this huge hill you should spare a thought for the hapless Spanish soldiers who fled this way after escaping the battle of Glenshiel on June 10 1719.

Start A87, Glen Shiel **(GR991132)**
Distance 4km (2½ miles)
Time 3½ hours
Height gain 1217m
Terrain long steep mountainside, narrow rocky ridge and steep summit cone.
Difficulty very strenuous
Popularity quiet

Route Zigzagging is a good way to get up this hill, but however you do it you should head NNW from the road until you top out on Sgurr na Ciste Duibhe (sister number one). Descend W then NW down the main ridge to a col at the head of Coire Dhomhain. From the col the ridge turns N and you follow it over Sgurr na Carnach (sister number two) to Sgurr Fhuaran (sister number three).

3 ACHNANGART ROUTE

A handy access route to the middle of the main ridge – useful if you need to quit the main ridge.

Start Achnangart, Glen Shiel **(GR962151)**
Distance 3km (2 miles)
Time 3-3½ hours
Height gain 1145m
Terrain steep-sided glen, long steep mountain side, narrow spur, narrow rocky ridge and steep summit cone
Difficulty very strenuous
Popularity quiet

Route Climbs steeply NE from the floor of Glen Shiel to gain the spur that runs NW from the summit of Sgurr na Carnach. Once on the crest of the spur you should follow it directly SE to Sgurr na Carnach. From the summit descend N to over a col then up the crest of the steep main ridge to Sgurr Fhuaran.

4 SGURR AN T-SEARRAICH ROUTE

A direct route onto the Five Sisters that gains the western end of main ridge via the fine little peak of Sgurr an t-Searraich. If you want to do all of the Five Sisters you will have to backtrack to do Sgurr na Mòraich, but this detracts little from a fine route.

Start Shiel Bridge **(GR934191)**
Distance 6km (3¾ miles)
Time 4 hours
Height gain 1297m
Terrain rounded ridge, broad col, rounded spur, narrow rocky spur and steep summit cone
Variation you can reach the col on the SE side of Sgurr an t-Searraich by a direct ascent from the eastern end of Loch Shiel

PAUL MILLIGAN

Difficulty strenuous
Popularity quiet

Route From Shiel Bridge climb the west ridge of Sgurr an t-Searraich to the top then descend SE to a broad col. From there climb the west ridge of Sgurr nan Saighead to join the crest of the main ridge, which you then follow SE to Sgurr nan Saighead's summit (fourth sister). Descend the main ridge SW to Bealach Buidhe. From the col climb the crest of the ridge SW then W to the top of Sgurr Fhuaran (third sister).

5 COIRE NA CRICHE ROUTE

A slightly more gentle approach to the main ridge but again, if you want to do all of the Five Sisters, you'll have to backtrack to Sgurr na Mòraich.

Start Ault a' chruinn (GR946203)
Distance 5.8km (3½ miles)
Time 3½ hours
Height gain 1166m
Terrain steep mountainside, hanging corrie, exposed col, narrow rocky ridge and steep summit cone
Difficulty strenuous
Popularity quiet

Route From the minor road at Ault a' chruinn follow the Allt a' chruinn SE past the waterfalls and up into Coire na Criche. Continue SE through the corrie then turn E and climb the head wall to gain the col on the SE side of Sgurr na Mòraich. From the col climb the steep narrow ridge SSW to gain the NW end of Sgurr nan Saighead's summit crest. Head SE to gain the main summit (fourth sister). Descend the main ridge SW to Bealach Buidhe. From the col climb the crest of the ridge SW then W to the top of Sgurr Fhuaran (third sister).

6 NORTH-WEST RIDGE OF SGURR NA MÒRAICH

This is the normal route of the main ridge after completing the traverse of the Five Sisters.

Start Carn-gorm (GR953206)
Distance 5.8km (3½ miles)
Time 4 hours
Height gain 1161m

Terrain steep mountainside, exposed col, narrow rocky ridge and steep summit cone
Difficulty strenuous
Popularity moderate

Route From the minor road climb the steep slopes S then SE to gain the rounded but more defined crest of Sgurr na Mòraich's north-west ridge, which you then follow directly to the top. From Sgurr na Mòraich's summit make the steady descent SE then S to the narrow col at the head of Coire na Criche. From the col climb the steep narrow ridge SSW to gain the NW end of Sgurr nan Saighead's summit crest. Head SE to gain the main summit (fourth sister). Descend the main ridge SW to Bealach Buidhe. From the col climb the crest of the ridge SW then W to the top of Sgurr Fhuaran (third sister).

7 EAST RIDGE OF SGURR FHUARAN

A superb narrow ridge that gives a long and airy approach to Sgurr Fhuaran. Doing this route negates being able to do all five sisters, but by heading south along the main ridge to Bealach an Lapain, you can create a superb horseshoe walk in its own right.

Start Morvich (GR959210)
Distance 10.5km (6½ miles)
Time 5 hours
Height gain 1063m
Terrain long, deep glen, long narrow ridge and steep summit cone
Difficulty strenuous
Variation direct start to the ridge from Glenlicht House
Popularity quiet

Route From Morvich follow the access track all the way down Gleann Lichd to Glenlicht House. Continue SE past the house for 1km then leave the path and make the steep climb SW onto the east ridge of Sgurr Fhuaran. Follow the crest of the ridge direct to Sgurr Fhuaran's summit.

8 GLEANN LICHD ROUTE

An heroic route that gains the eastern end of the Five Sisters ridge by a long trek along Gleann Lichd. It's a particularly useful approach if you don't have access to transport at both ends of the ridge. The north-eastern side of the main ridge is particularly impressive and is ample reward for a few extra miles' walking.

Start Morvich (GR959210)
Distance 14km (8¾ miles)
Time 6 hours
Height gain 1382m
Terrain long, deep glen, steep corrie, exposed col, narrow rocky ridge and steep summit cone
Difficulty strenuous
Popularity quiet
Route From Morvich follow the access track all the way down Gleann Lichd to Glenlicht House. Continue SE past the house then follow the Allt an Lapain S and make the steepening ascent to gain the Bealach an Lapain. From the col make the steady climb W along the crest of the main ridge over Sgurr nan Spainteach to the first of the Five Sisters – Sgurr na Ciste Duibhe. Descend W then NW down the main ridge to a col at the head of Coire Domhain. From the col the ridge turns N and you follow it over Sgurr na Carnach (sister number two) to Sgurr Fhuaran (sister number three).

"I've climbed it"

Roger Warland,
Tavistock

Last year my son Mark and I set off to climb Sgurr Fhuaran, the highest of the Five Sisters. With spirits high, we began slogging up the 40-degree slopes. By mid-morning I was beginning to lose my good sense of humour and feeling the effects of my hearty Scottish breakfast!

Eventually, Mark pulled me over the crest of the ridge to conclude what felt like one of the most gruelling mornings of my life! However, my spirits were soon rejuvenated by fine views of The Saddle and The Cuillins of Skye, as we traversed the ridge. At 4pm we reached the summit of Sgurr Fhuaran.

Much to my horror, my son then suggested that we complete the entire five peaks. In spite of the weather closing in and my morale slipping to an all-time low, I agreed. We triumphantly reached the fifth and final peak at 7pm. We had conquered the Five Sisters of Kintail.

Andy Ockelford,
Ireleth-in-Furness

As cultivated climbers and walkers, the choice of the Five Sisters for the weekend sounded sublime. However, as most of our outings involved wind, rain and no views, we expected just that – wind, rain and no sisters.

We started out on a sunny Saturday from the Cluanie Inn and traversed the ridge, descending just west of my favourite Scottish mountain, Sgurr Fhuaran, due to wind and driving rain.

To say the walk is classic is an understatement and, though it's not technically difficult, the views are outstanding and the sense of achievement is on a par with the ridges of Glencoe and Crib-goch. The Five Sisters of Kintail come highly recommended, although only the chosen few are promised, if not the whole ridge, at least a view!

Ian Thompson,
Wirral

Our unorthodox ascent of Sgurr na Mòraich was a killer – unrelentingly steep – but we were rewarded by incredible views in all directions when we topped out.

The ridge was terrific and seemed to go on forever. Each summit was achieved with a mixture of exhaustion and elation. Then, after the initial scramble, the descent off Sgurr nan Spainteach to Bealach na Lapain was a gentle end to the Sisters – lovely. The summit of Saileag now seemed very close, so we dragged ourselves to the top, had supper and then wearily followed its long northern ridge into the glen, to meet the stalkers' path through Gleann Lichd.

It was almost dark when we slaked our thirsts on water from the stream in the glen and started the long march to the Youth Hostel at Glen Affric. On arrival we collapsed onto our bunks for a well-earned kip at the end of the best mountain day I have ever had.

BOB ATKINS

LOCATION	**TORRIDON**
HEIGHT	**3049m (10,000ft)**
ACTIVITY	**10,000ft TRIP**

Facts

10,000ft trip

Why bother?

 Because climbing 10,000ft takes you around a huge amount of hill

Because nothing tastes quite as good as a 10,000ft pint

Because failure can be success – you'll learn about your limits and see some great places along the way

Which location?

We chose Torridon for its sheer scale

Checklist

Lightweight camping kit, ambition and a decent level of fitness

Mountains, Torridon style. High on Beinn Eighe with Liathach behind.

HAPPINESS IS PEAR-SHAPED

FROM FAILURE CAME FORTH FULFILMENT.
THE OVERAMBITIOUS **BEN WINSTON** CELEBRATES
A TRIP THAT WENT A WEE BIT PETE TONG.

PHOTOGRAPHY MATTHEW ROBERTS

Maps don't have clouds on them, nor do they show snow. And, as far as I know, maps don't take responsibility for the routes you plot on them. What they do, however, is allow the ambitious and dull-witted to plan itineraries that have no bearing whatsoever on reality, dreaming routes where streams are crossed with a leap of the fingers and inclines ignored because the eyes are firmly focused on the summit height above. Maps are of course blameless, being mere sheets of paper, but that's not to say a little warning box with something profound (Overambition is the wellspring of disaster) or merely prosaic (The hills are bigger than you) wouldn't go amiss. Even if such sensible advice wouldn't have stopped me trying to climb 10,000ft over a long weekend – an almost reasonable challenge without unseasonal winter and a full backpack – it might have made me think. It might also have avoided that embarrassing moment when, at the beginning of the end of our short first day in Torridon, Matthew the photographer asked the inevitable:

"Do you think we might have bitten off more than we can chew?"

"No. Definitely not. No, Matthew, we have definitely not bitten off more than we can chew. It'll be fine. Absolutely fine. Fine fine fine fine fine. Now just follow me..."

I knew he didn't believe me, what with being sandwiched between the vast bulk of Beinn Eighe and the awesome cliffs of Liathach, the packs ludicrously heavy and the distance on the map bearing no relation to the time it was taking us to walk it. We were trying to climb Beinn Eighe (pronounced *ay*) and a couple of remote northern Corbetts, thereby achieving a victorious 10,000ft of ascent and taking in some of the most incredible scenery to be found in the British Isles. But the sensation of 'way out there', both literally and in light of our aspirations, was beginning to make itself felt. The magnitude of our task was slowly dawning on us in the gathering dusk. That vast place, up in the far north of Scotland, felt as wild and exposed as nowhere else I have seen in this country – a feeling only exacerbated by the fact the mobile phone, that old get-out-of-jail-free card, hadn't had reception for over four hours. That's how lonely Torridon is.

For some unknown reason, that evening I was driven like a bull and bent on reaching Coire Mhic Fhearchair before darkness set in. I should have taken things easier and soaked up the awesome ambience, the strange rounded boulders of ancient sandstone and the little shards of icefalls hanging from Liathach like a thousand swords of Damocles. But ambition was burning and there was nothing in heaven or hell that could stop me dragging Matthew on up through the growing gloom, the weird light and eerie stillness creating an atmosphere of ghostly dislocation and vague hallucination, the heat

Contender for wild campsite of the year? Perched beneath Ruadh-stac Mór looking out towards Carn na Feola.

and sweat of an uphill struggle baking my brain like a pressure cooker, the increasing exhaustion, the unexplained things at the edge of my vision, the walk turning into a stagger, the feeling of floating, of moving without effort, the dull pain in my lower back, the sensation that we were nearly there, that it couldn't be much further now, that it had to be just around the bend, that the pain in my back was not really getting worse, no, that we could not stop because we were very nearly there, very very nearly now, just a few more steps, just... ARGHHHHHHH! With a snap in my back a burning pain floored me. I was in agony, and I writhed on the spot as a strange internal voice – audible only in times of folly or emergency – piped up the refrain: "He's fluffed it. He's fluffed it you know. He's *really* fluffed it. It's all over now."

It's an old adage that we pay for our mistakes, which perhaps makes it unfair that by the following morning the pain had receded to a dull ache. Still cocooned in my sleeping bag I discovered I could bend at the waist, so I sat up and peered out of the tent at a sight that instantly banished any doubts I had about being there. Camped right on the lip of the corrie, the view before me had an edge-of-the-world air about it, the ground falling away just a few metres from the tent and reappearing hundreds of feet down; a vast expanse of moorland scooped into a landscape of

daunting age. It was a place that looked ancient enough to shelter dinosaurs, such was its air of prehistory. But prehistory doesn't make breakfast and so, now deeply in love with Torridon, I slithered from the tent to put the stove on.

Crunching on the half rehydrated disaster that in theory was rice pudding (manufacturer to remain anonymous), Matthew and I looked at our options in the cold light of day. Aside from the problem of injury, it was becoming apparent that there is some disparity between the English spoken in England and the English spoken north of the border – our contact in the Highlands had clearly said: "Aye, there's just a wee sprinkling of snow on the tops" and yet here before us was a

mountain range in the full grip of a stubborn winter. A snow ramp led up our proposed gully and snow covered the tops. What with that, the weight of our sacks and my back, it was clear that our 10,000ft ideal was going to have to be abandoned.

The tent shrank to a tiny yellow speck as we climbed towards the summit of Ruadh-stac Mór, the higher of the two Munros on Beinn Eighe. It was hard ascending snow the consistency of margarine but the foot-swallowing saved us the effort of crampons, if not the need for an ice axe. Slowly we crept up the side of the corrie. The lake below was half frozen, the white edge of the ice etched into the black depths of the water in a zigzag pattern where small icebergs had broken off

A fine Beinn Eighe day.

and drifted across to the waterfall. Both it and our fabric home, the only visible indication of humanity, took on the toytown proportions you usually see from an aircraft. Although it was hard work, the recently forgotten clock of metres was ticking away.

Ruadh-stac Mór sported a view of the ridge that put the scale of our enterprise into perspective. Crusted in white, we realised our dream of ascent would have been an undertaking of near-Alpine proportions, the distant pinnacles of Sgurr an Fhir Duibhe clearly a stiff winter challenge that would have been impossible enough in their own right, let alone with the weight of the full rucksacks. Exploring Beinn Eighe with a day walk was clearly the best option. This realisation left us with a feeling of vindication that added a certain spice to the ecstasy of being up there in the first place, high in a frozen world completely devoid of other people and so utterly distant from the crazy rat race of everyday life. We settled down to munch on a second breakfast, watching the curious effect the centre weather system had as it settled upon Torridon: the clouds stopped moving, the wind died and the mountains lucky enough to have caught an early sunbeam looked like they might have that golden privilege for much of the day.

The ridge leading along to Spidean Coire nan Clach, the second of Beinn Eighe's Munros, offered more entertainment than I could have hoped for in a lifetime. The drops off the screes, although not steep enough to turn a slip into a terminal tumble, left the mind with the reeling sensation of being surrounded by more air than terra firma. It only got better (or worse, depending on your disposition), as we skirted the tops of cliffs plunging down into the northern corries where great banks of snow proved that, a breakdown in linguistic

Moving cautiously on the top of Triple Buttress, a 1,000ft plummet to Coire Mhic Fhearchair just beyond.

The view from the breakfast table.

That's a happy man, that. With the tops of Triple Buttress behind.

consensus regarding the words 'wee' 'sprinkling' and 'snow' notwithstanding, our contact had been seriously misinformed. It was absurdly beautiful though, even if the going was tricky – our crampons, while at home on the frozen crust, skittered and twisted on the rocks that poked through. The scrape of metal on rock was not entirely dissimilar to fingernails on a blackboard and this, coupled with the reward of a long plummet for complacency, made the ridge an extended grating of both teeth and nerves.

With a stiff scramble and a short razor arête of fine snow, the Spidean was ours. The landscape was frozen in time, the random patchwork of sunbeams stage-lighting Torridon to startling effect. In a giddy moment of elation, I uttered a wee squeak of delight. Matthew was suitably captivated too, this being his first day of winter Munros.

After the elation it came home to us once again that we had failed. We had not made it along the ridge, we hadn't peeped over the 10,000ft contour, and we were not going to backpack our way around Torridon. But the curious thing was, we just didn't care. We had discovered happiness and satisfaction with how far we had come, and had been rewarded with a stunning peak. I decided that if this is the price of failure then I want more of it – great vistas of low achievement and summits of catastrophe. I want to be a permanent flop.

As we made our way back towards the tent the clouds began to move. The weather system was ambling off like a lazy grey elephant, persuaded by a gentle breeze from the east. Sunbeams were also moving, washing the landscape and sparkling off the mirror shine of snow to pull distant mountains out of the gloom. Then, without warning, Liathach received the star treatment as a shaft of light poured down. It was a moment of sheer magic.

By the time we reached the tent our friendly weather system had been blown way out to sea and the

The clearest summit of the day.

Heaven comes to those who wait.

wind was banging and howling down the valley like a banshee. We moved the tent to a place of relative shelter but still spent the night listening to a roar like that of a jet engine. If possible, it was lonelier and more remote than ever thanks to the isolating influence of heavy weather, but with plenty of warm food and clothes coupled with the satisfaction of a great day's walking, comfort was well and truly ours.

Dawn found us huddled beneath scudding clouds, sleep having been hard to find amid the nightmares of being lifted airborne and floated unceremoniously down to the valley. We skipped breakfast in an effort to bail out of what was rapidly becoming a storm, and set off back to the car just as the rain began to patter, then turned to great sheeting buckets. Like drowning rats we were driven from the hills and back down to the road.

After a sneaky fry-up that boosted morale more than cold muesli and a wet tent

could ever have done (failure always being best achieved in style, we reasoned), we set out to complete part two of our original plan. Meall a' Ghiubhais and Ruadh-stac Beag were a couple of Corbetts plonked in the middle of the lonely lands north of Beinn Eighe which had promised fine views of our route, as well as what we had once considered valuable metres of re-ascent.

As it turned out the views, after we had climbed through the incredible pine forests of the Mountain Trail, were rather glum. The rain had moved on but the cloud had settled and our Corbetts provided one of those classic claggy hill moments – the sort of ascents that beg the question 'why?', but also the sort of ascents you end up looking back upon with a certain nostalgia.

The Corbetts were, for that afternoon, what I know as pub peaks: hills that add flavour to the pint and satisfaction to each single crisp. But they were also what I call setting-the-world-to-rights peaks: hills that could stop genocide, civil wars and

international trade disputes if only world leaders took the time to sink into the unique meditation offered by seven hours of cloud.

When we emerged we were of course in tranquil mood, but knackered. The Beinn Eighe National Nature Reserve had returned us to our wild roots for a few days and taught us never again to underestimate the size of a hill.

In the pub that evening I extracted the sodden remains of a map from my pocket. It had weathered the three days badly and resisted my attempts to restore it to its former glory with the aid of the radiator. It was beyond saving. So, with a fine dinner of venison pie being served as I faffed, thousands of feet-worth of contours refusing to unmush and fold neatly, I gave up, thinking bugger it – maps are only for people who want to know where they're going anyway. And with that, I tossed the remains into the fire.

The end.

LOCATION
ACTIVITY

GLEN COE
**Getting to know the UK's
most impressive valley**

Facts

Glen Coe

What's involved?
Getting to know
the UK's most
impressive valley

Why bother?
Because there is
more fun to be
had in these few square
miles than in most of
the rest of the country

Where?
Scotland's
Central Highlands

Checklist
A sense of adventure, a
head for heights and the
willingness to return again
and again and again...

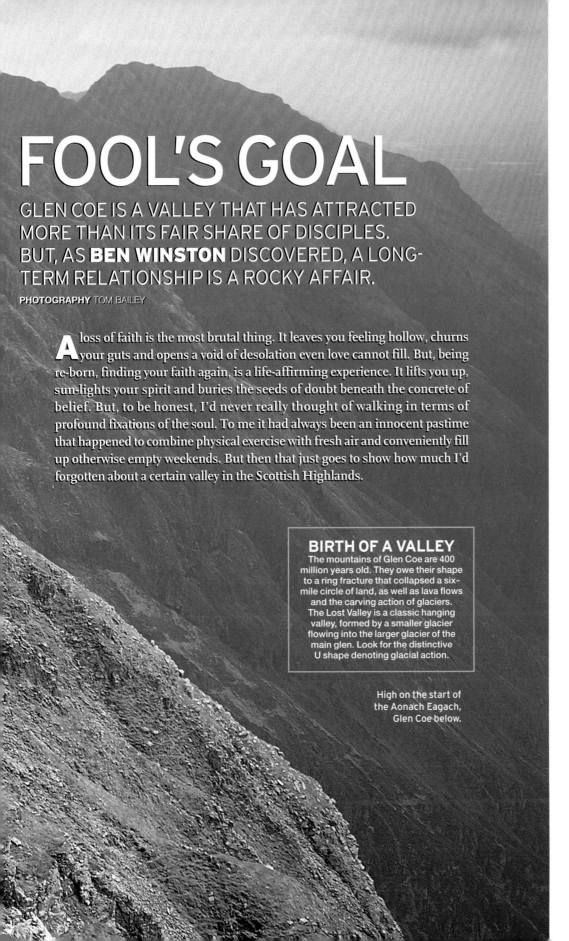

FOOL'S GOAL

GLEN COE IS A VALLEY THAT HAS ATTRACTED
MORE THAN ITS FAIR SHARE OF DISCIPLES.
BUT, AS **BEN WINSTON** DISCOVERED, A LONG-
TERM RELATIONSHIP IS A ROCKY AFFAIR.

PHOTOGRAPHY TOM BAILEY

A loss of faith is the most brutal thing. It leaves you feeling hollow, churns your guts and opens a void of desolation even love cannot fill. But, being re-born, finding your faith again, is a life-affirming experience. It lifts you up, sun-lights your spirit and buries the seeds of doubt beneath the concrete of belief. But, to be honest, I'd never really thought of walking in terms of profound fixations of the soul. To me it had always been an innocent pastime that happened to combine physical exercise with fresh air and conveniently fill up otherwise empty weekends. But then that just goes to show how much I'd forgotten about a certain valley in the Scottish Highlands.

BIRTH OF A VALLEY
The mountains of Glen Coe are 400 million years old. They owe their shape to a ring fracture that collapsed a six-mile circle of land, as well as lava flows and the carving action of glaciers. The Lost Valley is a classic hanging valley, formed by a smaller glacier flowing into the larger glacier of the main glen. Look for the distinctive U shape denoting glacial action.

High on the start of
the Aonach Eagach,
Glen Coe below.

People have often told me Glen Coe is the most awesome valley in the UK. "Don't question or quibble," they said, "it's a fact. Ask the director of *Highlander* or the location teams for *Braveheart* or *Rob Roy*. Ask the producers of adverts, postcards and calendars, or the walkers and climbers who go there. Everyone will tell you the same thing – Glen Coe is the most varied, exciting, dramatic, challenging, accessible and unforgettable valley in Britain."

But I didn't need convincing. I already knew. I have been playing in Glen Coe for as long as I've known the outdoors. My introduction to big mountains began there. In fact, between the ages of 15 and 22 I thought Scotland *was* Glen Coe because, other than the occasional trip to Fort William and the Ben, in five years of walking and climbing I never went anywhere else. I spent my time enthralled by the stories of famous mountaineers in the Kings House and the Clachaig, or climbing the delectable ridges of Buachaille Etive Mór. I learnt what it is to underestimate the mountains on a two-day traverse of the Aonach Eagach (it's a day walk). It was in Glen Coe that the mountains taught me all my lessons the hard way, camping through frozen winters and surviving on sheer naïveté, the odd pint of beer and plain good luck. So it is special to me and I looked forward to returning. But things never work out as you expect.

The pilgrimage began in the very bottom of the Glen. We were on our way to Bidean nam Bian, the valley's most elusive and well-protected mountain that hides behind a virtual maze of rock walls, remote corries and spectacular ridges. It is one of the most dramatic and complicated bits of upland architecture in the country, which means it should have been fun. Unfortunately the hot and humid weather made it grim instead, and the clouds had smothered the hills in a thick gruel. It was the sort of weather best endured with a cool bath and a long drink, but at that point I was still glad to be walking, looking forward to the only Glen Coe summit I had never reached.

The Lost Valley, er, lost.

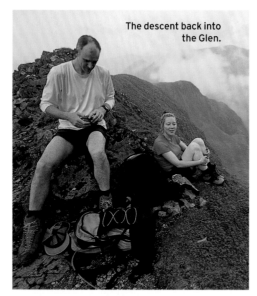

The descent back into the Glen.

We climbed towards the Lost Valley, sweat dribbling down our necks and turning T-shirts into sodden dish rags. But there were distractions: the smell of early-morning bracken, the baby wrens playing among the rowan, alder and beech. There were ferns that uncurled their leaves like tiny branches of a Mandlebrot set, and the almost luminescent contrast of a pink dog rose among the greenery. And, once we pulled over the lip into the hanging valley, we found a dried lake bed of stones looking like a giant Zen garden.

But the visual entertainment was short-lived and a few metres further up the valley we started to bore into the cloud.

Why is it that when you're in a good mood and the world looks rosy? Why do the bad times seem indistinct and unreal? Conversely, why, when bad moods make things looks hopeless and lost, do good memories become distant and unreachable? I was pondering this as I toiled up that hill high above the Lost Valley, black mood brooding, heading for the summit ridge. My limbs were as heavy as the atmosphere, which felt like a leaden balloon. It was disgusting. But even worse was the sensation that we were achieving nothing, gaining height slowly and being rewarded with an uninspiring view of thick cloud and disparate boulders beneath our feet. It was the ultimate in awful mountain experiences. Fetid, still weather and a depressing fog that had somehow entered my brain. Why on earth was I doing this? I was hating every minute.

I held out hope for a breath of wind when we reached the ridge, but none materialised. I also held out hope for some form of summit elation on the top of Stob Coire nan Lochan, but that remained elusive too. In fact, it was as we toiled up the last few metres to this inappropriately named 'top', a summit where I have cried tears of elation and screamed happiness with all the power of my lungs on a beautiful solo winter's day, that the penny dropped. Walking is stupid. Mountains are for fools. And with that, my previously sacred belief dropped into the gooey pool of truth and sank without a trace. I stared after it, feeling hollow, but saw just swirling mist. A huge part of my being had gone.

Glen Coe, how could you do this to me?

Lunch was a sorry affair. I stared forlornly at bread that tasted stale and munched half-heartedly on some sweaty cheese. I'd have to find a new life now, I thought: something that doesn't involve mountains. I'll sell my boots and my fleece, pawn my compass and take up, oh, I don't know... making matchstick replicas of the Mary Rose?

A breeze gusted over the summit but my head was down and I was staring at the stones. I hardly noticed it. Then the cloud thinned and cleared a little, but I missed that too. It wasn't until it was time to move on that I stood up and looked around to find Glen Coe coalescing out of the mist. Way, way down beneath my feet was Coire nan Lochan; and, turning clockwise, the Lost Valley. Then the distinctive ridges that run into Glen Coe like massive slugs of rock and, at their far end, Buachaille Etive Mór. I chanced a little smile. Spinning slowly, there was the view to Glen Etive still obscured in fog and then, dramatic and standing tall and proud, the Bidean herself. Awesome.

The things people do for fun in the mist.

Ascending to the Lost Valley.

Stob Coire nam Beith's north face comes through the mist.

"The ridge dropped into a roller coaster of five-star thrills, scrambling above enormous drops on fantastic rock... fearsome arêtes and pinnacles."

We followed the ridge from Stob Coire nan Lochan to the Bidean, then on around to Stob Coire nam Beith. The cloud cleared properly and the Aonach Eagach appeared on the other side of the valley, then the Mamores beyond it and finally, faintly, Ben Nevis itself. I was warming to walking once again, feeling the exposure of the cliffs that fell away in a complex series of walls and gullies beneath our feet; enjoying the show of cloud that spilt over Beinn Maol Chaluim to the south and hung irresolutely in the valley of Fionn Ghleann to the west. There were patches of sunlight appearing, roaming the Highlands, and the breeze had driven away the humidity to leave a freshness in its wake. It was turning into a beautiful afternoon.

By the time we came to descend to the Clachaig, the sun was burning, the sky was blue and faith had returned to my wobbly legs. The black mood and doubt of earlier felt like a memory from another world and the foundations of my outdoor existence were once again shored up against despair. Belief, that old friend in times of adversity, had been resurrected and now shone like a neon cross, flashing gaudily on the hillside of my soul. And, like a hovering angel or a challenge to my resolve, the Aonach Eagach loomed above. "Tomorrow..." I promised myself.

The Aonach Eagach is one of the classic days out in Britain. It's a bit like Crib Goch, after a session in the gym. The scrambling runs to Grade 3 and many a gibber has been had on its pinnacles where the ground falls away. It is not a route to underestimate. But at age 16 and with a rucksack full of shiny new kit, danger and difficulty don't look the way they do when (and if) you reach adulthood. Which is why years ago, because of the happy accident of not having enough money to go to the Alps (where we would have met with certain death), my best friend and I completed the only known two-day, siege-style, 25 kilo rucksack traverse of the ridge. We hadn't planned it that way, but enthusiasm, incompetence and an innocence about mountain weather, forced us to overnight on Meal Dearg. We were lucky – we got a cloud inversion at sunrise. And the next day, when we ran out of water, it was innocence that made us break the most sacred rule of surviving the Aonach Eagach and descend off its side.

Years later and it was a very different story. We had day sacks, started from the Clachaig Inn and not the Devil's Staircase, and rocketed straight up the path beside the gully. The weather had decided to stay clear although again it was hot and muggy, but by the time

High on the gentle Sgorr nam Fiannaidh, beginning or end of the Aonach Eagach.

BUACHAILLE ETIVE MÓR

'The Buachaille' is Glen Coe's most famous mountain. Greeting people on their entry to the valley, it sports two Munros and some classic UK scrambles such as the Crowberry Ridge and Curved Ridge. Also home to the famous 'Rannoch Wall' – one of the valley's best climbers 'playgrounds.

AONACH EAGACH
A UK classic. One of the best ridge scrambles in the country, taking in two Munros and some exposed and exciting scrambling. The pinnacles provide the crux but there are plenty of razor arêtes, slabs, corners and cracks to keep your interest up.

Welcome to the drop (but it's not the crux!).

Glen Coe to the furthest horizon.

Aonach Dubh, one of the Three Sisters.

we were standing at the top, Glen Coe and the Aonach Eagach stretching out before us, a breeze was massaging discomfort away. And I was elated. Twenty four hours earlier, I had thought it was all over, but now I was born again, gazing down at the river dancing with the A82 along the floor of the glen, the Three Sisters leading the eye to the Buachaille, then, beyond, the hazy prospect of Rannoch Moor with diamonds glinting in its countless mini lochs. It's a magical place, Glen Coe, capable of making you feel the most incredible things.

From the top of Sgorr nam Fiannaidh the ridge dropped into a roller coaster of five-star thrills, scrambling above enormous drops on fantastic rock and through fearsome arêtes and pinnacles. I was grinning the whole way, putting every inch of my being into the movement, the handholds, the foot placements, the cracks and corners and slabs that led us through the most amazing scramble in the valley.

But halfway along I had the strangest experience. I was 16 again and on my first trip to Glen Coe. Young, irresponsible and plucky, with a false belief of invulnerability inspired by the weight and variety of equipment on my back, I was discovering the big mountains for the very first time. It was incredible – the length of that drop and the way my hair stood involuntarily on end; my ability to control the fear and keep moving when everything inside me said, "Stop! Freeze! You're terrified." I looked at the size of the Bidean opposite; I'd never seen anything so huge in my life. And I looked over towards Ben Nevis and thought I'd like to climb that some day. Then I took note of the world beyond the valley and saw the

Highlands and realised that they offer a lifetime of fun." I knew that mountains are what it's all about and had that tingling feeling of elation that comes when you know, deep down, that something is profoundly right.

By the time we reached Am Bodach I was apoplectic with joy, blathering like a fool. The Aonach Eagach had restored in a few fateful hours that which had been lost in the fog of yesterday's dejection. And all those non-walker's questions that had haunted me so recently – 'Why do you bother?', 'What's the point of climbing a long, tiring hill?' – were answered. Not by the simple: 'because it's there', but because climbing mountains brings you from the 'there' to the very real 'here and now'. And that is what Glen Coe does better, more dramatically and with more variety than any other valley in the UK.

As I stood on that final summit, gazing down on the valley responsible for so much of my past and so much of what makes walking in Britain great, I had one of those strange moments of lucidity. I knew then that for as long as I live I'll be returning to Glen Coe to accept its challenges, to repeat its classics, to drink and tell tall tales in the comfort of its pubs. I knew that it would continue to abuse my faith with its fits and strops of bad weather, but I also knew there would also be ample reward.

And I knew that one day I'll take my kids there, and my kids will take their kids there, and my family will join the countless other families who have experienced joy and trauma there, adding our struggles and achievements and tragedies to the long story that is Glen Coe: a unique, timeless and very special place.

Who needs captions?
The expression says it all.

Facts

Ridge scramble

What's involved?
▲ Blurring the distinction between scrambling and climbing, with a heck of a view under your heels

Why bother?
▲ Trust the rock, push your limits, and free your mind

Where?
▲ Skye – it's a Mecca for scramblers

Checklist
climbing gear; confident scrambling technique and a head for heights

Ben gets big air on the summit ridge of Sgurr Dubh Mór.

Hot-wire the soul

TAKE A BONNIE BOAT TO SKYE AND SUCCUMB TO INSTANT SCRAMBLING ADDICTION.

WORDS MARIA DEL CARMEN CLEGG
PHOTOGRAPHY BOB ATKINS

There's a ridge on Skye which scythes its way from sea-level to black volcanic mountain tops – and it could just be the best scramble in the UK. The Dubhs (pronounced doos) Ridge is rated as a Grade 3 scramble / Moderate climb, but that's just technical talk. The Scottish Mountaineering Club's *Skye Scrambles* gives the route the highest 'thrill' rating – three stars for its spectacular location, the quality of rock and sustained sequence of moves along it.

You just know it's going to be a good trip.

A traverse of the famous Cuillin is a major expedition: a day carrying water to strategic 'drops'; a high bivvy; complex terrain with subsidiary ridges to trick you off the route. It's a big gamble which doesn't always come off. The Dubhs Ridge, by way of contrast, is a challenging classic scramble without all the organisational hassle. Just over two kilometres long, with 944m of total ascent, the Dubh is the longest scramble in the UK. The route rises from the south-western shore of Loch Coruisk, over a series of broad rock slabs at a fairly steady 30 degree angle, then dives headlong into twisting crags and gullies to spit you out on the summit ridge of the Cuillin, the most spectacular mountain range in the UK.

To get there, we chartered a boat from Elgol, a fishing village tucked away on Skye's south-western coast. This would take us practically to the doorstep of the Coruisk Memorial Hut, our base camp for the next few days. It had struck me as an extravagant way to travel – maybe this is how Posh and Becks would get to the hut if they went scrambling for a few days – but sharing the cost between us gave us a better deal than you ever get with public transport, and it meant that we could take all the things that

don't usually make it on a backpacking trip: books, a real towel, icebox...

Donald MacKinnon, the owner of the boat, used to fish these waters, taking visitors on boat trips from Elgol as a sideline in the summer months. Before long Donald and his wife Bella realised that the sideline offered them a better future than fishing ever could. So, ten years ago, they threw their luck in with the visitors who come to see Skye in mist and driving rain, and the lucky few who see the island in brilliant sunshine. The rucksacks which lay in multicoloured chaos on the spotless decks were packed with our walking gear for the trip, but spiced with the climbing kit we'd need on the route. Once unpacked at the hut, we explored the bay that would be our home for the next few days. I walked five minutes around the coastline and looked out to sea, grateful for the peace after a long day spent travelling.

I sat for a while, letting go of the mundane. The late evening sun sent a million stars skittering across the sea, as I waited for dusk to fall. Picking up the path back to the hut, I walked past two red deer feeding quietly, indifferent to the rise and fall of excited conversation and the cooking smells drifting on the still air.

We started our big day with a gentle amble to the start of the route. The Dubhs Ridge begins in a lovely spot half an hour's walk from the hut along the shore of Loch Coruisk. I'd realised a long time ago that I was no rock-climber. A case of sewing machine leg, top-roped, ten feet up a gritstone crag convinced me of that. As I see it, climbing involves a tenuous grip on existence itself, only a 9mm rope and a couple of measly bits of metal – laughingly called friends – between you and an impromptu chorus of hallelujahs from a heavenly choir. But scrambling? Love it. Three points of contact, nice big handholds, clambering over boulders, with time to look at the views as well. So, in a style most generously described as 'plucky', I made my move on to the route. A couple of easy hand- and foot-holds led up a steep crag to an early crux, high enough from the rocky ledge below to give an authentic 'been through the cheese grater' feeling in the event of sliding off.

I warily eyed the crux from the security of my ledge. It was interesting, in the way that poking coat hangers into electrical sockets is interesting. I cupped a hand over a rounded lump of sun-warmed rock, pushing up on the precarious foothold, but the next moves flowed easily underneath my hands and feet, and I soon joined the rest of our group on top of the crag. We put on harnesses, which we roped into at odd moments during the day for confidence on the trickier moves, and helmets to protect from the rockfall which any one of us could trigger.

The next couple of hours were spent in an unhurried ascent of the overlapping slabs and easy blocky scrambles along jagged faults in the rock strata. Scrambling is a liberating experience. It empties the overflowing wastepaper bin of your mind, throwing out all those mental Post-its, and To Do lists. Random thoughts are filtered out until your entire body is working

Down-scrambling,
Skye-style. Abseiling
off Sgurr Dubh Beag.

Top left: "What do the tea leaves say...?" Top right: Slab happy. Bottom right: Claws for concern over Maria's lunch. Bottom left: "What a boot-iful day!"

on the problem that really matters: can I reach that hold, could I stand on that edge, and where do I go from there?

More than this, scrambling on Skye is addictive. There are as many reasons for this as there are Skye scrambling addicts, but you can guarantee that a trip to the island hot-wires your soul. The stark, age-old beauty did it for me. Rock and sea to the horizon; pinnacles and buttresses, U-shaped valleys and sweeping corries, carved out over hundreds of millions of years by the extremes of fire and ice.

Ten thousand years ago, the Cuillin was covered in a sea of ice over a mile thick, but the main peaks along the elegantly curved ridge would have risen steeply from it like an archipelago of volcanic islands, and the jagged towers of the ridge which resisted the sweep of the icy high tide were splintered again by frost to give the island its rakish profile.

This is a landscape that can capture your imagination in a million different ways, and it's so different in character to other British mountains that it really has to be seen to be appreciated. But if you think Skye looks good from a distance, you won't believe what it's like when you're on it.

Up close, Skye is the stuff of dreams; the Cuillin lays claim to possibly the grippiest climbing surface in the world – gabbro. This coarse-grained volcanic rock is so much fun to climb on, it should be illegal. You can run up the stuff like a cat up a curtain. You can choose an easier line over the slabs or pick a 'climbier' route. It's all going the same way anyway, and it's your call. Well, do you feel lucky?

We gained Sgurr Dubh Beag – little black peak – almost effortlessly, and looked back along the route, past the curved ridge leading way back down to the Coir'-uisg valley floor, and poured scorn on the Red Cuillin's rounded contours. The only way to experience the world was 'three points of contact' up, or 'look away now if you don't want to lose your dinner' down. Anything in between just wouldn't do.

The route off Sgurr Dubh Beag was an exhilarating abseil, and only the merest hint of sweaty palms and a brief episode of incoherent pre-takeoff babbling betrayed the adrenaline coursing through me, making even the ends of my fingertips tingle.

This interlude took us to the foot of the summit ridge of Sgurr Dearg Mór – the big black peak. This slender spine seems to be made almost entirely of Skye air but there is, here and there, enough rock for you to walk along.

If you're picnicking in Skye wear a harness.

If you can bear to tear your eyes away from the square blocks at your feet, you're rewarded with a panorama of the main Cuillin ridge. A jagged flake of rock with an improbable rock face demands closer attention. This spectacular sight in the middle of the Cuillin ridge is the K2 of Munros: Sgurr Dearg, or the Inaccessible Pinnacle. This Munro is hard – so hard it throws eggs at cabinet ministers and thumbs its nose at policemen – and the reason it's so hard is that it is the only one classified as a rock-climb. Munro-baggers, take note!

From the summit ridge, we dropped over a col on the summit ridge of Sgurr Dearg Mór – at 944m, the highest point of our route – to snowplough through soft, knee-deep snow to Coir' an Lochain, and on to the boulder field.

Threading a twisted route down the chaos of rock, we followed the sporadic cairns, which were becoming more indistinct now we were walking in shadow. We had left the hut ten hours ago, but we had a heck of a walk-out ahead of us. Behind us, the sun still picked out the snow in the high corrie we had descended, dazzling against the black pinnacles, but the ground in front of us was a poker face. The rest of our descent lay

Skye return trip guaranteed.

somewhere in among the jumbled rocks and overlapping slabs that tumbled away out of sight. We picked a route carefully around cliffs, retracing our steps a couple of times when a duff line led us to the top of a sheer precipice, finally picking up a faint path threading downstream to Loch Coruisk.

The rest of the walk-out was an unrelenting grind over rough terrain, which we covered as quickly as we could to add some kind of interest. Back at the hut, we took turns to stir the pasta, and, in between celebratory sips of whisky from chipped mugs, relived the slabs, the abseil and the airy ridges, and made tentative plans for our last full day at Coruisk before sinking into gabbro dreams.

On our morning of departure, we lazed by the landing stage as we waited for Donald and Bella's boat to take us back to Elgol. My knuckles were scratched from being jammed inside narrow cracks; fingerprints had long since disappeared, rasped away on the rough rock, and I ached all over from sheer physical effort. Skye, eh? Makes you glad to be alive.

One for the album – Sgurr Dubh Mór souvenir summit shot.

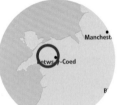

Y Lliwedd

Despite a height of 898m and perfect mountain proportions, Y Lliwedd doesn't always get the attention it deserves. Though its ridges and peaks are in all the right places, it is overshadowed somewhat by its glamorous neighbour Snowdon, which attracts an estimated half a million people a year. Such celebrity status may draw the masses, but the relative few who visit Y Lliwedd realise that it, too, is worthy of the limelight.

Wild and graceful, it rises into three elegant peaks, with a gigantic face. At 370m it's the highest cliff in the UK outside the Scottish Highlands. Starved of sun during the winter months, the barren slopes can resemble the dark side of the moon, but there is beauty in this stony wasteland. The bleakness drops away into crags and

gullies, where streams gather momentum. Like blue veins they pump life into the wilderness, tumbling via magnificent waterfalls into the lakes that lie in the cwms.

The massive north face gives some classic hemp'n'hobnails easy climbs, and in winter is the domain of the experienced mountaineer. But Y Lliwedd is ideal for winter hill-walkers too, offering classic rocky, narrow ridges and exhilarating scrambles with stunning backdrops. It's an old-fashioned, traditional mountain and a climber's playground.

The 1953 Everest team trained here, in their bid to secure the summit of the world's highest peak. They stayed in the Pen-y-Gwryd Hotel at the foot of the Llanberis Pass, which has long been associated with the mountaineering establishment. The area provided the type

IT MAY LIVE IN SNOWDON'S SHADOW, BUT THIS HANDSOME
WELSH MOUNTAIN HAS PLENTY OF CLAIMS TO FAME...

Words **Jane Baker**

of terrain encountered on Everest, but without the altitude. Initial oxygen trials were done at nearby Nantgwynant, the cylinders making revolutionary use of technology developed in World War Two. Led by Colonel John Hunt the team included Edmund Hillary and George Band, the trips were as much an exercise in group bonding as planning for the ascent.

Surviving members of the 1953 Everest expedition hold reunions at the hotel every five years. It's a welcome place to go for a pint after a hard day out on the hills. You can breathe in a little inspiration too – souvenirs bought back by the team are on show in a glass case and include an ice axe, a boot, goggles and the payroll book detailing the Sherpas' wages. Take a look up at the ceiling of the Everest Room, which is covered in the signatures of top mountaineers including Hillary, Bonington, Brasher and Tenzing Norgay (you're drinking in esteemed company).

Long before their time, another group of mountain buffs met regularly in the area. Led by the bohemian educationalist Geoffrey Winthrop Young, they compared the climbing here to that of the Alps. Young, who was a passionate mountaineer, was born into privilege and in later life founded the British Mountaineering Club. During World War One, he lost a leg to shellfire; but he continued climbing with the aid of a prosthetic limb. In the early 1900s he established the infamous Pen-y-Pass parties. University types including the likes of George Mallory would meet at a hotel for supposed reading weeks, but romped up the mountains instead.

The landscape was very different then. By modern standards the bowl of Snowdon around Glaslyn would have been considered an industrial estate rather than a national nature reserve. The flanks of Y Lliwedd were littered with copper mines employing over 200 men, and today their tracks remain etched into the hillside. They laboured deep within the belly of the mountain extracting precious copper ore, much of which was used to protect the bottoms of ocean-going ships. There would have been a cacophony of noise which is hard to imagine now, walking along the Miners' Track. But the remains of the crushing rooms still stand, an echo of a humble past. Some open mine shafts remain too around Glaslyn, so do remember to take care when you're next walking in this area.

Blue slate was also mined from Y Lliwedd. Indeed, the Watkin Path, named after Sir Edward Watkin, the man who built it, is a continuation of the tracks leading from the quarries. This is the only route on Snowdon constructed specifically to allow tourists to

reach the summit and it was opened in 1892 by the 84-year-old Prime Minister William Gladstone. He gave a rallying speech to the 300 or so people who'd gathered to hear him. Despite their initial enthusiasm historic records suggest that only two of them actually made it to the summit. A huge boulder, known as the Gladstone Rock, near the path at Cwm Llan, commemorates the event with a descriptive plaque.

Y Lliwedd has also achieved celluloid fame, playing an important role in the 1968 comedy *Carry On Up the Khyber*. For fans of the film the location is at **SH624517**. So to get a slice of the action, pull on your walking boots and head west to discover Y Lliwedd, the 'last nail in the Snowdon Horseshoe'.

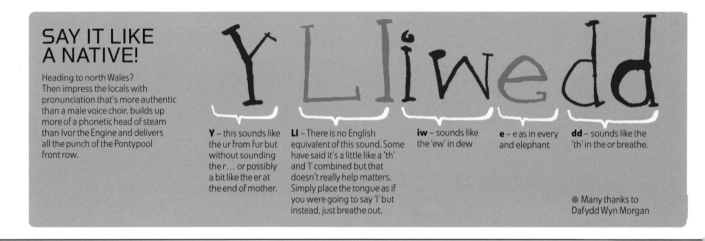

SAY IT LIKE A NATIVE!

Heading to north Wales? Then impress the locals with pronunciation that's more authentic than a male voice choir, builds up more of a phonetic head of steam than Ivor the Engine and delivers all the punch of the Pontypool front row.

Y – this sounds like the ur from fur but without sounding the r… or possibly a bit like the er at the end of mother.

Ll – There is no English equivalent of this sound. Some have said it's a little like a 'th' and 'l' combined but that doesn't really help matters. Simply place the tongue as if you were going to say 'l' but instead, just breathe out.

iw – sounds like the 'ew' in dew

e – e as in every and elephant

dd – sounds like the 'th' in the or breathe.

● Many thanks to Dafydd Wyn Morgan

the routes
● The times given are for the walk to the summit only – not there and back.

1 Y GRIBIN

Y Gribin is the pronounced spur which extends NE from Snowdon's SE ridge. It climbs high above Glaslyn and offers a short but exciting scramble.

Start Pen-y-Pass (**SH647557**)
Distance 5.5km (3½ miles)
Time 2-2½ hours
Height gain 541m
Terrain rocky slopes, craggy corries, steep rocky ridge and narrow summit ridge
Difficulty strenuous (Grade 1 scramble, Grade 1 winter climb)
Popularity moderate

Route From Pen-y-Pass take the Miners' Track S, W then SW to Llyn Llydaw. Cross the Causeway, follow the track SW around the lake then turn W up to Glaslyn. Cross the Afon Glaslyn and climb the grass-and-rocks slope SW onto the shallow col. From the col climb the crest of the ridge SW onto the levelling on the SE ridge of Snowdon. Turn L and follow the main ridge SE to the summit of Y Lliwedd.

2 NORTH-EAST RIDGE

The quickest way up Y Lliwedd – the main descent of the 'Snowdon Horseshoe walk'.

Start Pen-y-Pass (**SH647557**)
Distance 4km (2½ miles)
Time 2 hours
Height gain 541m
Terrain rocky slopes, craggy corries, steep rounded ridge and narrow summit ridge
Difficulty intermediate
Popularity busy

Route From Pen-y-Pass take the Miners' Track S, W then SW to Llyn Llydaw. Before the Causeway turn L off the track and follow the path which climbs the steep rounded ridge SSW towards Lliwedd Bach. Turn R and follow the main ridge SW to the summit of Y Lliwedd.

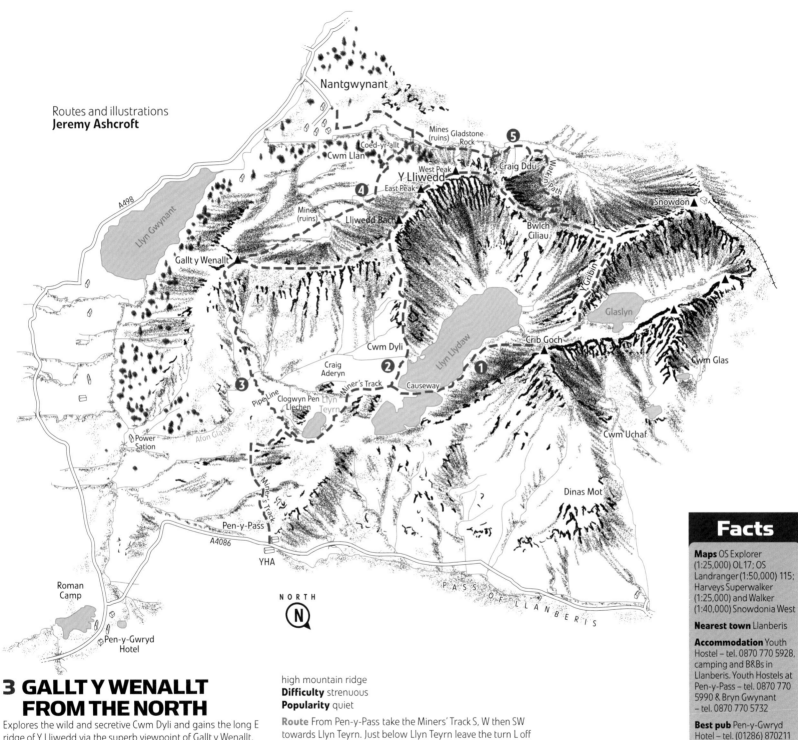

Routes and illustrations
Jeremy Ashcroft

3 GALLT Y WENALLT FROM THE NORTH

Explores the wild and secretive Cwm Dyli and gains the long E ridge of Y Lliwedd via the superb viewpoint of Gallt y Wenallt.

Start Pen-y-Pass (SH647557)
Distance 4.5km (2¾ miles)
Time 2-2½ hours
Height gain 640m
Terrain rocky slopes, boggy corrie, steep rocky slopes and high mountain ridge
Difficulty strenuous
Popularity quiet

Route From Pen-y-Pass take the Miners' Track S, W then SW towards Llyn Teyrn. Just below Llyn Teyrn leave the turn L off the track and descend S towards Afon Glaslyn. Cross Afon Glaslyn and climb the long steepening slope SSE to gain the main ridge on the E side of Gallt y Wenallt. Turn R and follow the crest of the ridge W over Gallt y Wenallt then SE to the summit of Y Lliwedd.

Facts

Maps OS Explorer (1:25,000) OL17; OS Landranger (1:50,000) 115; Harveys Superwalker (1:25,000) and Walker (1:40,000) Snowdonia West

Nearest town Llanberis

Accommodation Youth Hostel – tel. 0870 770 5928, camping and B&Bs in Llanberis. Youth Hostels at Pen-y-Pass – tel. 0870 770 5990 & Bryn Gwynant – tel. 0870 770 5732

Best pub Pen-y-Gwryd Hotel – tel. (01286) 870211

4 GALLT Y WENALLT FROM THE SOUTH

A remote and devious route up the southern flank of Y Lliwedd that gains Gallt y Wenallt via the abandoned mines of Cwm Merch.

Start Nantgwynant **(SH627506)**
Distance 6km (3¾ miles)
Time 2½-3 hours
Height gain 828m
Terrain steep-sided valley, steep slopes, hanging corrie and high mountain ridge
Difficulty strenuous
Popularity quiet

Route From the A498 at Nantgwynant take the lane N to the start of the Watkin Path. Join the path and follow it as it weaves its way NW to a junction on the upstream side of the Coed-yr-allt waterfalls. Take the R branch and follow the path NE up into Cwm Merch. Past the mine workings climb the steep hillside ENE to Gallt y Wenallt. From Gallt y Wenallt head SE along the crest of the main ridge to the summit of Y Lliwedd.

5 WATKIN PATH

The product of a dedication by Sir Edward Watkin and opened by Gladstone on 13 September 1892, the Watkin Path climbs a logical route up the head wall of the wild and lovely Cwm Llan.

Start Nantgwynant **(SH627506)**
Distance 6km (3¾ miles)
Time 2½ hours
Height gain 828m
Terrain woodland, huge crag-ringed corrie, steep head wall, exposed col and narrow summit ridge
Difficulty intermediate
Popularity busy

Route From the A498 at Nantgwynant take the lane N to the start of the Watkin Path. Join the path and follow it as it weaves its way NW over a bridge and past the Gladstone Rock into Cwm Llan. Through the spoil heaps at the abandoned quarries the path turns NE then N and climbs the steep head wall to Bwlch Ciliau. At the col turn R and follow the main ridge SW to the summit of Y Lliwedd.

We can see you!
Y Lliwedd peeps over
Cribau's shoulder, with
Glaslyn and Llyn Llydaw
to the left.
TOM BAILEY

"I've climbed it"

Philip Hall Redditch

Three friends – Beardy, Nicholl and 'GPS' Bob – horseshoed their way around Snowdon, then boasted about the terror of Crib Goch, spectacular views of the Pass of Llanberis and the tough slog of Y Lliwedd. All this torment was aimed at Gooch and I, who decided to escape to north Wales.

Nearing the Pen-y-pass car park the area became covered in a Welsh mist. At the Bwlch y Moch saddle we peered southwards for a glimpse of Llyn Llydaw; it was a blank white canvas. The path became an uphill struggle for me, but Gooch (who must don a Spiderman costume at night) pulled effortlessly upwards on invisible webs. We were met by the prehistoric ridge, which looked like a spiny-backed dinosaur, asleep in a sulphury swamp. The three pinnacles loomed like ships' bows from a fogbank and we scaled them. Momentum from the gentle grassy downhill of Crib y Ddysgl carried us up to the Snowdon summit.

On our descent the track suddenly disappeared and Silva's searching needle seemed confused. After scanning for landmarks the mist gave us its blankest look yet and there was nothing else for it but to take the high ground. We were stationary, treading uphill on a downward-moving fine-scree escalator. Eventually we gained the ridgeline and dropped out of the mist to see the comforting causeway crossing.

Steve Ward Nuneaton

On a very windy February day, five of us did the Grade 1 scramble up onto Y Lliwedd. The gale almost stopped us and we found we could lean right into the wind without toppling.

Ascending the east ridge, we estimated the wind to be reaching 70 mph plus and had to stop, cling to the rocks in a huddle, then as it dropped, run towards the next small outcrop of rocks. We did this until reaching the flanks of Y Lliwedd.

We didn't hang around though, and went straight down the ridge ; eventually we could talk to each other without shouting!

Despite only fleeting visits to the two summits and a howling gale, this was a great afternoon's entertainment.

Elidir Fawr

Rate it or slate it, this most modest of mountains has more of a tale to tell than many of its famous friends.

Words **Piers Pickard**

The Ogwen Valley Glyderau are the show-offs of the British hills. They crowd around Llyn Ogwen and Llyn Idwal flexing their muscles, letting everyone admire the Castle of the Winds, the Cantilever Stone, Bristly Ridge and the Devil's Kitchen. But there's one mountain that doesn't preen with them. Elidir Fawr sits alone to the west of the main group. It's not body-beautiful like Tryfan or Glyder Fawr. It is more retiring, more modest.

But don't be put off by the disfigurations left by quarrying. Look past the fact that the summit is sandstone and shale, not granite. Take a closer look at the peak the other mountains turn their backs upon and you'll discover it has its own talents and a quieter, more private charm.

For wide, open vistas west across the Irish Sea and stretching north to the Menai Straits, there is no finer top in Snowdonia. In the other direction the view of the western peaks of the Ogwen Valley (Carnedd y Filiast, Mynydd Perfedd, Foel-goch and Y Garn) shows them to be softies when sneaked up on from

Elidir Fawr: way out west.
JEREMY ASHCROFT

behind, with broad-backed grassy slopes undulating along from north to south, easily attainable by a short hop over the Bwlch y Brecan.

The mountain's northern slopes hide some surprising secrets. Underneath Marchlyn Mawr reservoir is hidden a 1,680 megawatt pump-storage power station. This was the largest in the world when it was built in 1984 at a cost of £450 million. But don't camp too near the shore because when electrical demand is low, the six turbines are reversed and water is pumped back uphill from Llyn Peris to refill the reservoir. You could wake up floating away on your Thermarest!

LOCATION	SNOWDONIA
HEIGHT	923m (3,028ft)
SUMMIT GR	611612

High above Marchlyn Mawr the cliffs of Craig Cwrwgl (Coracle Crag) contain other secrets. Here, where climbers rarely bother to come, is the much-coveted Pillar of Elidir, an impregnable-looking pinnacle standing free from the northern flank of the mountain. There's also the classic Hard Severe 'Corrugated Cracks'; but these routes see much less traffic than those on Tryfan and the other 3000ers clustered around Llyn Idwal a few miles to the south-east.

The huge slate quarries of Llanberis dominate the whole of the west side of the hill. The Caernarfonshire Slate Belt, as it is known, contains the largest slate quarries in the world; so even if you think it is an ugly thorn in the beautiful side of Snowdonia, remember that the workings were providing employment and a source of income for locals long before tourism arrived.

The south of the mountain offers the best approach from the Llanberis side. The Dudodyn valley is deep-sided, as though cowering back from the ugliness of the quarries below. Its tumbling brown waters seem to have laid out boggy areas deliberately to ward off man's approach, but the sheep tracks lacing the valley sides always provide a way around them.

Elidir Fawr isn't flash and extrovert like its Glyder neighbours. It's more of a loner, keeping its back to the others while they show off their famous faces to all and sundry. But as the most westerly of the 3000ers, it has charms of its own. So don't pander to the clamouring of its better-known brothers; give the quiet guy some attention, and you'll have the reward of seeing Snowdonia from a new angle.

The defunct Dinorwic slate quarries scar the flanks of Elidir Fawr.

THE PHOTOLIBRARY WALES/©RAY WOOD

the routes
● The times given are for the walk to the summit only – not there and back.

1 CWM DUDODYN PATH

A long but pleasant ascent through the verdant interior of the south-facing Cwm Dudodyn.

Start Nant Peris **(GR606584)**
Distance 5.2km (3¼ miles)
Time 2½-3 hours
Height gain 814m
Terrain steep pasture, steep-sided corrie and narrow rocky summit
Difficulty intermediate
Popularity moderate

Route From Nant Peris take the lane opposite the Post Office (PO) NE then NW to join a track. Continue generally NW along it as it climbs to the start of the Cwm Dudodyn Path. Follow the path as it zigzags up to the Afon Dudodyn. The path follows the Afon Dudodyn NE, first on the S bank then over a footbridge onto the N bank. Continue NE ascending the length of Cwm Dudodyn. At the head of the cwm turn NW and climb the very steep slope to Bwlch y Marchlyn. From the col climb the narrow ridge WSW to the summit of Elidir Fawr.

2 SOUTH FLANK

This is an unremitting slog from the mouth of Cwm Dudodyn to the south-west end of Elidir Fawr's summit ridge. This route probably serves best as a descent.

Start Nant Peris **(GR606584)**
Distance 3.6km (2¼ miles)
Time 2½ hours
Height gain 814m
Terrain steep pasture, steep-sided corrie, rocky ridge and narrow rocky summit
Difficulty intermediate
Popularity moderate

Route From Nant Peris take the lane (opposite the PO) NE then NW to join a track. Continue generally NW along it as it climbs to the start of the Cwm Dudodyn Path. Follow the path as it zigzags up to the Afon Dudodyn. The path follows the Afon Dudodyn NE, first on the S bank then over a footbridge onto the N bank. Continue along it to the mouth of Cwm Dudodyn proper then make the steep ascent NW up the south flank. As the summit ridge is reached, turn NE. Scramble easily up the crest to the summit cairn.

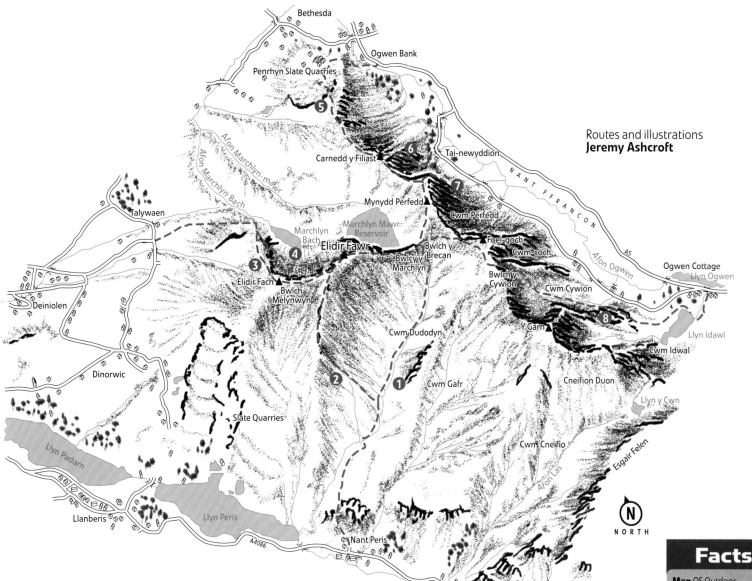

Routes and illustrations
Jeremy Ashcroft

3 NORTH RIDGE

Climbs directly up the north ridge to the subsidiary peak Elidir Fach then gains Elidir Fawr via the expansive col and scree slopes of Bwlch Melynwyn.

Start Talywaen **(GR594631)**
Distance 3.6km (2¼ miles)
Time 2 hours
Height gain 601m
Terrain moorland, rocky corrie, rounded ridge, high open col, scree and narrow summit ridge
Difficulty easy
Popularity quiet

Route From the road take the Marchlyn Mawr Reservoir access road SE to the junction below Marchlyn Bach Reservoir. Leave the road and ascend the ridge S to Elidir Fach. From the summit head SE and cross Bwlch Melynwyn to make the short but steep ascent to the summit ridge of Elidir Fawr. On the ridge turn NE and scramble easily up the crest to the summit cairn.

4 NORTH FLANK

Works a circuitous but interesting line to Elidir Fawr's rocky summit by skirting the top of Cwm Marchlyn's dark and secretive crags.

Start Talywaen **(GR594631)**
Distance 3.6km (2¼ miles)
Time 2-2½ hours
Height gain 591m
Terrain moorland, rocky corrie, rounded ridge, scree and narrow summit ridge
Difficulty intermediate
Popularity quiet

Route From the road take the Marchlyn Mawr Reservoir access road ESE to the junction below Marchlyn Bach Reservoir. Leave the road and ascend the ridge S towards Elidir Fach. As the angle of the ridge eases **(GR605620)** contour SE then E to the edge of the crags of Cwm Marchlyn. Before the edge is reached turn S (in mist or snow this can be difficult to judge – so turn early) and climb the steep scree to Elidir Fawr's summit ridge. On the ridge turn SW and follow the crest to the summit cairn.

What lies beneath Elidir Fawr's rugged exterior?

5 NORTH RIDGE OF CARNEDD Y FILIAST

This route climbs directly up the skyline crest of Carnedd y Filiast then gains Elidir Fawr, the subsidiary top of Mynydd Perfedd and the exposed col of Bwlch y Brecan.

Start Ogwen Bank (**GR627654**)
Distance 6.5km (4 miles)
Time 2½-3 hours
Height gain 731m
Terrain wooded valley, slate quarries, steep ridge, high mountain ridge, exposed col and narrow summit ridge
Difficulty intermediate
Popularity moderate

Route Cross the Afon Ogwen and follow the track NW to the entrance of the quarry workings. Turn S and follow the path as it works its way up through the Penrhyn Slate Quarries onto the north ridge of Carnedd y Filiast. Climb the crest of the ridge to the summit of Carnedd y Filiast then head SSE to Mynydd Perfedd. Descend SW to Bwlch y Marchlyn. From the col climb the narrow ridge WSW to the summit of Elidir Fawr.

6 ATLANTIC SLAB

A top-end scramble high on the wild crags of Carnedd y Filiast overlooking Cwm Graianog.

Start minor road near Tai-newyddion (**GR632634**)
Distance 4.1km (2½ miles)
Time 2½-3 hours
Height gain 790m
Terrain steep-sided valley, hanging corrie, steep arête, high mountain ridge, exposed col and narrow summit ridge
Difficulty strenuous (Grade 3 scramble)
Popularity quiet

Route Climb the steep hillside SE into Cwm Graianog and gain the grassy ridge on the S side of the cwm. Climb the ridge until you are above the remains of a sheepfold in the bottom of the cwm. From this point it is easy to identify Atlantic Slab on the opposite side of Cwm Graianog. Directly above the boulder and scree fan (which extends from the lowest part of the crags to the wall) is a huge tilted slab – Atlantic Slab. The route climbs the broken R edge of the slab. Contour round the cwm and up the scree fan to the lowest point of the slab. Follow the crest making the odd move L to avoid difficulties. As the top of the slab is reached the angle relents and the scrambling becomes easier. Gain the summit of Carnedd y Filiast then head SE to Mynydd Perfedd. Descend SW to Bwlch y Marchlyn. From the col climb the narrow ridge WSW to the summit of Elidir Fawr.

The summit of
Elidir Fach (visited
on route 3).

JEREMY ASHCROFT

7 SOUTHERN RIDGE OF CWM GRAIANOG

A classic rocky arête that climbs steeply onto the broad col between Carnedd y Filiast and Mynydd Perfedd. An easier alternative out of Cwm Graianog if you don't fancy Atlantic Slab.

Start minor road near Tai-newyddion (**GR632634**)
Distance 3.6km (2¼ miles)
Time 2½ hours
Height gain 770m
Terrain steep-sided valley, hanging corrie, steep arête, high mountain ridge, exposed col and narrow summit ridge
Difficulty strenuous (easy scrambling)
Popularity quiet

Route Climb the steep hillside SE into Cwm Graianog and gain the grassy ridge on the S side of the Cwm. Climb it S until it steepens to the base of the southern bounding ridge of Cwm Graianog. Climb its narrow crest SW onto the col between Carnedd y Filiast and Mynydd Perfedd. Head SE along the main ridge to Mynydd Perfedd. Descend SW to Bwlch y Marchlyn. From the col climb the narrow ridge WSW that takes you to the summit of Elidir Fawr.

8 CWM CYWION ROUTE

Climbs through the remote and little-visited Cwm Cywion and provides a handy route from the Ogwen Valley.

Start Ogwen Cottage (**GR650603**)
Distance 5.6km (3½ miles)
Time 2½-3 hours
Height gain 664m
Terrain broad craggy corrie, mountain lake, steep rocky slope, high open corrie, rounded mountain ridge, exposed col and narrow summit ridge
Difficulty intermediate
Popularity quiet

Route Take the Cwm Idwal path SE then SW to Llyn Idwal. Cross the footbridge at the NE end of the lake and follow the vague path which snakes up to the base of the NE ridge of Y Garn. Before the base is reached, leave the path and contour NW into Cwm Cywion. Continue NW up through Cwm Cywion and ascend the head wall to Bwlch y Cywion. From the col head NNW along the main ridge then turn W and traverse across the side of Mynydd Perfedd to Bwlch y Marchlyn. From the col climb the narrow ridge WSW to the summit of Elidir Fawr.

"I've climbed it"

Graham Steel King's Lynn

One bleak January evening, I was persuaded to attempt the Welsh 3000ers (within 24 hours) the following July. This coincided with the sad news that two pupils at the school where I teach had severe health problems – one a heart condition and the other leukaemia. Not wishing to miss a chance to stress to the other children the need to give help to those who need it in any way we can, I told them in assembly all about my plans; and they agreed to sponsor me a penny a peak from their pocket money, all money raised to go to a charity providing accommodation for families whose children are hospitalised for long periods.

So it was, having climbed Snowdon in the dark, scrambled along Crib Goch as the sun rose and breakfasted in Nant Peris, we faced the climb to Elidir Fawr. The cloud descended and visibility was poor. Until, that is, we neared the summit. As we paused for breath, we realised we had climbed above the cloud. We could see numerous peaks poking out of the steaming, milk-like fluffy stuff, flooding the valleys below. It was a magical moment.

After a short rest in the shelter of the summit rocks, we continued towards the remaining 11 peaks, visibility deteriorating with every step. It remained very poor for the rest of the day, but we did complete the route and raised £1,170 in the process. Elidir Fawr stands out in my memory of the day as the only spot where we had a decent view!
PS: Both children are doing well.

Robert Miles Portslade

The weather was giving us a mixed reception as we arrived at Ogwen. It looked promising but big rain clouds still floated around. Y Garn appeared and disappeared at will as our party of three intrepid mountaineers climbed the track to Cwm Clyd and on, following the crest all the way to the ridge just short of the summit. Turning away from Y Garn, we headed north along the main ridge now in a much brighter mist (the sun was up there somewhere). The cloud occasionally

cleared to give us stunning views down the Nany Ffrancon pass. Our route now turned west across the face of Mynydd Perfedd and it was not long before we attained the rocky summit of Elidir Fawr. It was then it happened. The sun suddenly broke through and the clouds just melted away and we stood in awe at the breathtaking scenery around us – it made our day. To save going back the same way, we called on the wonders of modern science (the mobile). A call was made and a car was arranged to meet us on the other side of the mountain (at the Vaneor Arms on Nant Peris). Just couldn't think of a better place to celebrate our day.

LOCATION	**BRECON BEACONS**
HEIGHT	**886m (2,906ft)**
SUMMIT GR	**GRO12215**

Pen y Fan

Looming over Brecon, this flat-topped people magnet is easily accessible – but don't underestimate it...

WORDS ED KENYON

M ountains, just like people, gain reputations over the years; some fearsome, others benign. Yet a mountain's reputation does not wane with the passage of time – it evolves with each new set of footprints left on its summit. Every fresh visit to its high ground touches somebody new and a bond is formed between person and mountain. Some peaks have that special magnetism which can draw the same people back to its flanks time and time again, while others fail to make that lasting impression. Pen y Fan undoubtedly has that magnetism.

If you've ever driven along the A470 towards Brecon then you'll have felt it. The main Beacons ridge, with Pen y Fan at the epicentre, rears up like a breaking wave suspended in time; its uncluttered ridgeline and long, sweeping slopes topped by stark table-topped summits of which Pen y Fan is the highest at 886m. You're hooked already. It doesn't take long.

Back in 1724, Daniel Defoe (of *Robinson Crusoe* fame) described this unique upland scene as "horrid and frightful, even worse than those mountains abroad." Almost three centuries on they provoke a more positive reaction, with Pen y Fan becoming one of the best known, and most trampled, mountains in the country. But what exactly is it that makes this grass-covered sandstone peak such an icon for so many hill-walkers?

All it needs is a cherry on top!

TOM HUTTON

Facts

Maps OS Outdoor Leisure (1:25,000) 11; OS Landranger (1:50,000) 160; Harveys Walker (1:40,000) Brecon Beacons; Harveys Superwalker (1:25,000) Brecon Beacons East

Nearest town Brecon

Accommodation hotels and B&B in Brecon; Youth Hostel at Llwyn-y-celyn – tel. (01874) 624261; camping at Llwyn-on Village

Tourist information Brecon – tel. (01874) 622485

As any well-versed estate agent will tell you, location is the key when it comes to houses; and so it is with Pen y Fan. It lords it over the Usk valley far beneath its northern flanks and casts a spell over the town of Brecon which lies in its shadow. The sheer northern cliffs of Pen y Fan and its near neighbours seem almost improbable when compared to the rolling upland scenery surrounding them. It is this individuality which marks them out for special attention.

Viewed from the south, Pen y Fan is a very different proposition. Smooth, grassy slopes extend gently up to what appears to be an unremarkable summit. It packs a weaker punch from this side. But that is the paradox of Pen y Fan. The walker approaching from the south and west can be lulled into thinking an ascent of this mountain is little more than a stroll. However, its smooth grassy coat, and its proximity to the area's roads, conceals a harder, highland edge.

Pen y Fan's summit might be as flat as a Fenland field, but it almost touches the 3,000ft mark. At that height the wind whips across with a ferocity scarcely imaginable from the safe confines of the wooded valleys below. There is no shelter up there. No rocks to hunker down behind and get a brew going. Throw in some thick cloud which can gather out of nowhere and Pen y Fan suddenly becomes a tougher proposition, as little Tommy Jones found out in 1900. The five-year-old got hopelessly lost after visiting his grandfather at Cwm-llwch Farm and succumbed to exposure on the featureless ridge of Craig Cwm Llwch. His body wasn't found for a month; an obelisk now marks the tragic spot.

The ability to use a map and compass is as relevant here as on any peak, despite the deeply scarred paths which criss-cross its flanks lending an impression of accessibility. You'll often see khaki-clad members of the armed forces tramping over its slopes, which are a supreme test to their fitness and navigation skills.

Yes, Pen y Fan has a mean streak, but that is not the abiding memory which stays with anyone who has reached its summit. It is the sheer splendour of the vista from its peak, the unlikely nature of its glacially-carved grassy precipices and the simple fact that there is no higher piece of land south of this in the UK. It's the diversity of the routes – smooth and gentle from south and west; steep and ridge-like from the north and east. But overall it's the satisfaction factor which really counts. No matter what time of day you're there, you cannot fail to be impressed by this Welsh 'Table Mountain'. At sunset there are fewer places a walker would rather be; but don't forget your headtorch and bivvy bag...

These hills were made for walking...

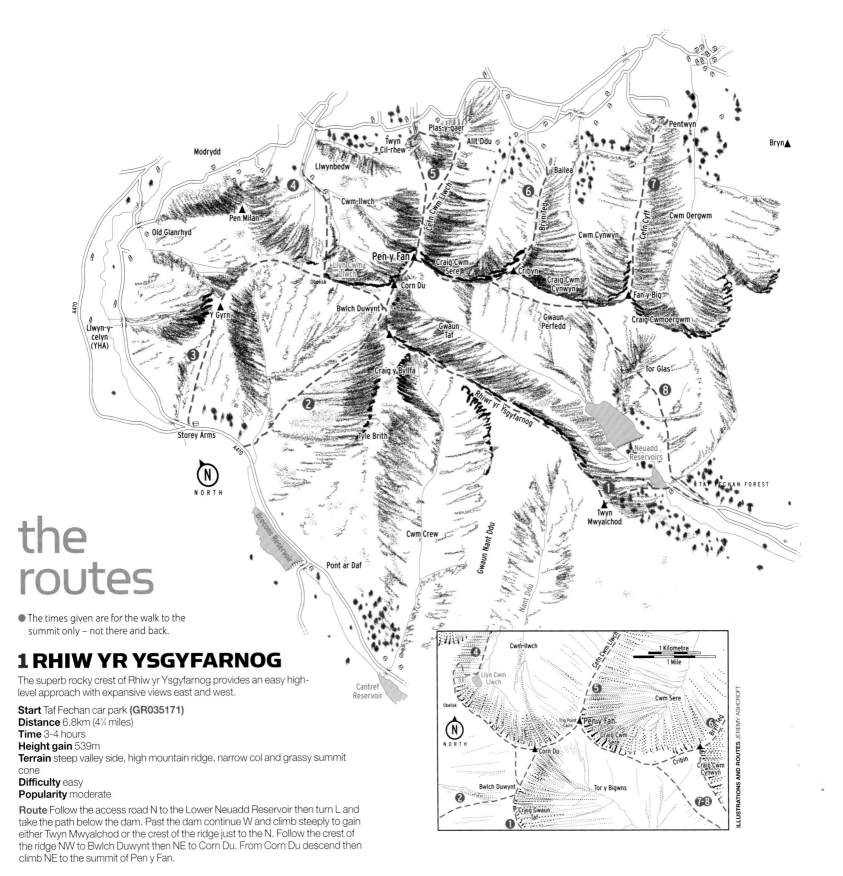

the routes

● The times given are for the walk to the summit only – not there and back.

1 RHIW YR YSGYFARNOG

The superb rocky crest of Rhiw yr Ysgyfarnog provides an easy high-level approach with expansive views east and west.

Start Taf Fechan car park **(GR035171)**
Distance 6.8km (4¼ miles)
Time 3-4 hours
Height gain 539m
Terrain steep valley side, high mountain ridge, narrow col and grassy summit cone
Difficulty easy
Popularity moderate

Route Follow the access road N to the Lower Neuadd Reservoir then turn L and take the path below the dam. Past the dam continue W and climb steeply to gain either Twyn Mwyalchod or the crest of the ridge just to the N. Follow the crest of the ridge NW to Bwlch Duwynt then NE to Corn Du. From Corn Du descend then climb NE to the summit of Pen y Fan.

ILLUSTRATIONS AND ROUTES JEREMY ASHCROFT

Cribyn's vast north face seen from the summit of Pen y Fan.

2 BWLCH DUWYNT

A very popular route – the shortest 'up and down'.

Start A470 car park at Pont ar Daf **(GR987198)**
Distance 3.2km (2 miles)
Time 2 hours
Height gain 490m
Terrain steep corrie, narrow col and grassy summit cone
Difficulty easy
Popularity very busy

Route From the car park take the path ENE past the forest plantation and cross the stream. Climb steeply E then NE up through the corrie to gain Bwlch Duwynt. From the col turn L and climb NE to Corn Du. From Corn Du descend then climb NE to the summit of Pen y Fan.

3 Y GYRN PATH

A popular route that gains the north-west ridge of Corn Du via the subsidiary top of Y Gyrn. It's a bit of a slog at first but once Y Gyrn is reached things become much more interesting with expansive views down Glyn Tarell and entertaining walking on the ridge above the big drops of Craig Cwm Llwch.

Start near the Storey Arms Centre **(GR982203)**
Distance 4.5km (2¾ miles)
Time 2 hours
Height gain 496m
Terrain steep mountainside, rounded summit, broad col, high mountain ridge, narrow col and grassy summit cone
Difficulty easy
Popularity very busy

Approaching the
Tommy Jones Obelisk.

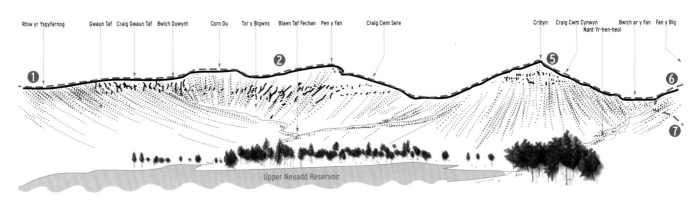

TOM BAILEY

Rhiw yr Ysgyfarnog   Gwaun Taf   Craig Gwaun Taf   Bwlch Duwynt   Corn Du   Tor y Bigwns   Blaen Taf Fechan   Pen y Fan   Craig Cwm Sere   Cribyn   Craig Cwm Cynwyn   Bwlch ar y Fan   Fan y Big

Nant Yr-hen-heol

① ② ⑤ ⑥ ⑦

Upper Neuadd Reservoir

Route From the W side of the Storey Arms Centre climb the steep path NNE to the summit of Y Gyrn. Continue NNE and make the slight descent to the broad col. From the col head E then SE to the obelisk at the base of the north-east ridge of Corn Du. Climb the crest of the ridge direct. From Corn Du descend then climb NE to the summit of Pen y Fan.

4 CWM LLWCH

An interesting approach via the pretty Llyn Cwm Llwch and the dour north face of Corn Du.

Start roadhead, Cwm Llwch **(GR006245)**

Distance 5km (3 miles)
Time 2½ hours
Height gain 654m
Terrain access lane, steep corrie, grassy mountain ridge and grassy summit cone
Difficulty intermediate
Popularitiy busy

Route From the roadhead follow the track then path as they climb steeply S into Cwm Llwch. On nearing Llyn Cwm Llwch the path zigzags W to gain the north-west ridge of Corn Du which you then climb SE to the summit of Corn Du. From Corn Du descend then climb NE to the summit of Pen y Fan.

Clambering up the top section of Pen y Fan's south-east ridge.

5 CEFN CWM LLWCH

A direct and uncompromising slog straight up Pen y Fan's north-east ridge (Cefn Cwm Llwch).

Start Cwm Gwdi car park **(GR024248)**
Distance 4km (2½ miles)
Time 2½ hours
Height gain 566m
Terrain steep corrie and grassy ridge
Difficulty intermediate
Popularity busy

Variation The W flank of Allt Ddu is crossed by a footpath that gains the N end of Cefn Cwm Llwch

Route From the car park follow the track W then S up through the shallow corrie on the W side of Allt Ddu to gain the northern end of Cefn Cwm Llwch. On the ridge follow its crest SSW to the summit of Pen y Fan.

6 BRYN TEG PATH

Bryn Teg, Cribyn's sweeping north-east ridge, follows a steep, narrow line and provides an elegant route on and off the main Brecon Beacons ridge.

Start Bailea **(GR038238)**
Distance 4.8km (3 miles)
Time 3 hours
Height gain 706m
Terrain steep grassy ridge, high mountain ridge, narrow col and grassy summit cone
Difficulty intermediate
Popularity busy

Route From the roadhead S of Bailea climb the crest of Bryn Teg direct to the summit of Cribyn. From Cribyn descend W to the broad col on the main ridge, cross it then make the final climb W then NW to the summit of Pen y Fan.

Looking north-west from Corn Du.

7 CEFN CYFF

Similar in character to Bryn Teg but longer and quieter, and it takes in the fine summit of Fan y Big.

Start Rhiwiau near Pen-yr-heol **(GR058241)**
Distance 7km (4¼ miles)
Time 3½ hours
Height gain 807m
Terrain steep grassy ridge, high mountain ridge, narrow cols and grassy summit cone
Difficulty intermediate
Popularity quiet

Route From the roadhead near Pen-yr-heol climb the bridleway then path SW onto the end of Cefn Cyff. On Cefn Cyff follow its crest SSW to the summit of Fan y Big. From Fan y Big descend W to Bwlch ar y Fan then climb W then NW to Cribyn's summit. From Cribyn descend W to the broad col on the main ridge, cross it then make the final climb W then NW to the summit of Pen y Fan.

8 NEUADD RESERVOIRS BRIDLEWAY

Climbs past the attractively set Neuadd Reservoirs along the course of a Roman road to gain the eastern end of the main Brecon Beacons ridge at Bwlch ar y Fan.

Start Taf Fechan Forest car park **(GR037171)**
Distance 6.5km (4 miles)
Time 2½ hours
Height gain 601m
Terrain forest, steep-sided valley, high mountain ridge, narrow cols and grassy summit cone
Difficulty easy
Popularity busy

Route From the car park take the access road NW to the start of the bridleway (Roman road). Follow the bridleway N as it climbs the hillside above the Upper Neuadd Reservoir to gain Bwlch ar y Fan. From the broad col turn L and climb W then NW to the summit of Cribyn. From Cribyn descend W to the broad col on the main ridge, cross it then make the final climb W then NW to the summit of Pen y Fan.

"I've climbed it"

Andy Wilkinson, Cardiff

We managed to get up Pen y Fan in 10 minutes! I'd taken a group of adults with learning difficulties away to the Beacons for two days. We'd spent the previous day helping the Rangers repair footpaths and were now about to walk up Pen y Fan. The summit was shrouded in mist and everyone was up for it – except one guy who wanted to know how much longer it was to the top.

"One hour," I told him. "Don't want to do one hour!" "How long do you want to do?" I asked. "Ten minutes," he replied. "Okay, 10 minutes it is," I said. With that he slipped his mittened hand in mine and we proceeded happily on our way, regularly checking it was still 10 minutes to the top. Pen y Fan gave us a fantastic day, providing both a challenge and a terrific sense of achievement for the group.

Jan Langmead, Brecon

I had decided not to use my torch so my eyes could accustom themselves to the dark – it was 6.30am on New Year's Day. I had seen the sun rise – or not, as is usually the case – from the summit of Pen y Fan every year for 16 years. I was feeling optimistic as I climbed to the rounded, stony plateau, and was greeted by a pale, orange sky glowing in the east. Suddenly a tiny segment of orange appeared, soon to evolve into a great ball of fire casting a magnificent golden hue on the surrounding hills. A dense, white mist snaked its way along the Usk valley. I could have burst into song; instead I devoured two mince pies and turned for home.

LOCATION	SNOWDONIA
HEIGHT	947m (3,107ft)
SUMMIT GR	631596

Y Garn

Always the outsider, it's time for this Welsh 3000er to enjoy its season in the sun.

O f all the seasons, summer is the one when we lay down memories to keep alive our mountain dreams through the short winter days. Y Garn is without a doubt a summer peak. The classic midsummer expedition known as the Welsh 3000ers – a traverse of Snowdon, the Glyders and the Carneddau massif – is for many people their first outing on this peak. Following the classic running order, starting with a summit bivvy on Snowdon, Y Garn is the fifth peak climbed, after Crib y Ddydgill, Crib Goch and Elidir Fawr, before the continuation of the route over the Glyders and Carneddau.

Y Garn from the Ogwen Valley – it's just a summer's day away.

Facts

Maps OS Outdoor Leisure (1:25,000) 17; OS Landranger (1:50,000) 115; Harveys Walker (1:40,000) & Superwalker (1:25,000) Snowdonia North

Nearest town Bethesda

Accommodation Youth Hostels and campsites in the Ogwen Valley

Tourist information Betws-y-Coed – tel. (01690) 710665

ROBIN ASHCROFT

143

With such an embarrassment of mountain riches, you might be forgiven for failing to notice Y Garn's subtle charms. It is one of those peaks rarely climbed for its own sake, and is more frequently the added spice in a long summer's day in the Welsh mountains, upon the happy realisation that there are more hours of daylight at the end of a planned route than you had hoped for. Indeed, Y Garn fits the bill exactly as the end to a perfect trip.

Though this peak enjoys a certain reflected glory from its inclusion in the Welsh 3000ers, it is an attractive and much under-rated mountain in its own right. It is almost perfectly pyramid-shaped, with four distinct faces. The peaceful corries on the north and east faces on the Ogwen Valley side more than repay the effort it takes to explore them, though caution should be exercised on the crags towards Foel Goch. The south and west faces flow in an elegant, unbroken line towards Llanberis. It is noteworthy that the corries on both the Nant Peris and Ogwen sides have a remote unvisited quality, despite the human traffic on the surrounding peaks.

An ascent of Y

Garn is most memorable for the climb up the long and graceful north-east ridge, and the views. Once gained, by whatever route you choose, the summit rewards the walker with one of the most wildly dramatic sights in Britain: a panoramic view of Tryfan, the Glyders, Pen yr Ole Wen, Carnedd Daffyd, and, of course, Snowdon. However, in foul weather, when the only view to be had is that of the inside of your drawn-up hood, it's possible to eat lunch sheltered from the worst of the weather by a walled windbreak.

Some would say that Y Garn is a better place for having been overlooked. Snowdon's longstanding popularity with daytrippers means that it can now boast a thoroughly ruined summit, most memorably described by Prince Charles as "the highest slum in Europe". Elidir Fawr, visible from Y Garn, is scarred by extensive slate quarrying on its western and northern flanks; and though the slate boom which allowed Llanberis to prosper for a time has passed, Elidir Fawr still has its shoulder to the wheel of progress. A series of underground vertical shafts and tunnels give it the nickname of Electric Mountain for its supply of peak demand power to the national grid.

In contrast, Y Garn is – give or take a little wear and tear on the north-east ridge – a pristine mountain. Its ecological importance was recognised when Cwm Idwal was designated the first Welsh National Nature Reserve. From April onwards, this high cwm and the crags around it host a silent firework display of arctic-alpine wildflowers, and the rugged corrie of Twll Du – the Devil's Kitchen – is one of the few places where the rare Snowdon lily grows. As Y Garn's wealth of bio-diversity makes abundantly clear, a quiet life is no bad thing.

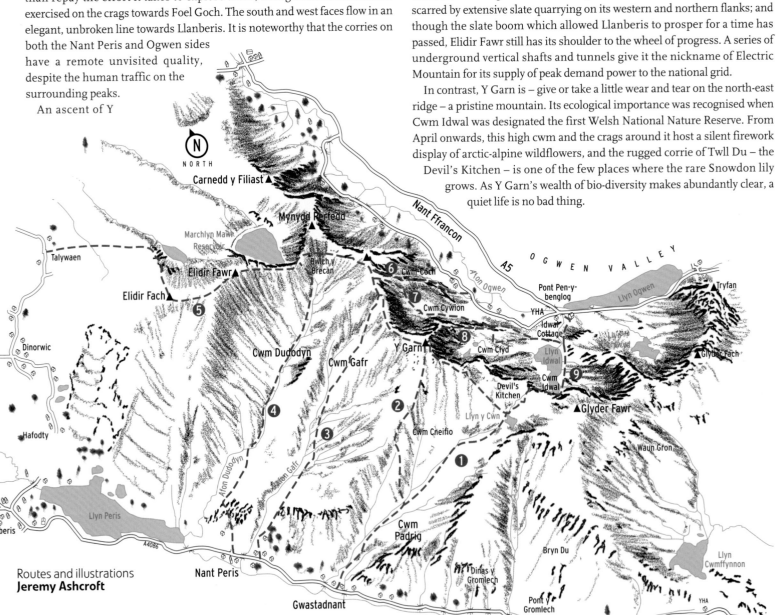

Routes and illustrations
Jeremy Ashcroft

Descending the north-east ridge from the summit.

the routes
• The times given are for the walk to the summit only – not there and back.

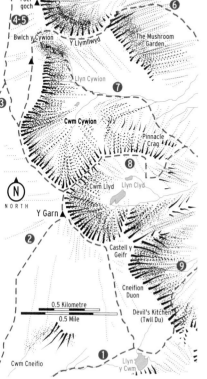

1 LLYN Y CWN PATH

A pleasant approach via the beautifully situated Llyn y Cwn on the south-east side of Y Garn.

Start A4086 near Gwastadnant **(GR615576)**
Distance 4km (2½ miles)
Time 2½ hours
Height gain 821m
Terrain steep pasture, steep open corrie, mountain lake, moderate scree-covered slopes and rocky summit
Difficulty easy
Popularity moderate

Route From the A4086 take the track then the path NE to the side of Afon Las. Continue NE up the path as it climbs alongside the course of the Afon Las, detouring slightly E to avoid the crags by the waterfalls to arrive at a broad col occupied by Llyn y Cwn. From Llyn y Cwn follow the main path NNW then NW up the summit slopes to the top of Y Garn.

2 SOUTH-WEST RIDGE

The South-West Ridge offers the most direct approach from the Llanberis side – useful as a descent route.

Start A4086 near Gwastadnant **(GR615576)**
Distance 2.8km (1¾ miles)
Time 2½ hours
Height gain 821m
Terrain steep pasture, steep open corrie, rounded mountain ridge, scree-covered slopes and rocky summit
Difficulty easy
Popularity quiet

Route From the A4086 take the track then the path NE to the side of Afon Las. Continue NE up the path as it climbs alongside the course of the Afon Las, detouring slightly E to avoid the crags by the waterfalls. Once above the waterfalls cross the Afon Las and climb N up the steep slopes onto the rounded crest of the South-West Ridge, which you climb NW to Y Garn's summit.

145

Y Garn and Foel Goch above Llyn Ogwen

3 CWM GAFR PATH

Climbs through the steep open corrie of Cwm Gafr directly from Nant Peris.

Start Nant Peris **(GR606584)**
Distance 3.2km (2 miles)
Time 2½ hours
Height gain 835m
Terrain steep pasture, steep-sided corrie, exposed col, high mountain ridge and rocky summit
Difficulty easy
Popularity quiet

Route From Nant Peris take the lane (opposite the post office) NE. At the sharp LH bend join the Cwm Gafr Path and follow it as it winds E through the buildings then NE up through Cwm Gafr. Near the top of Cwm Gafr turn E and climb to the col on the N side of Y Garn. From the col turn SE and climb the steep summit slopes to the top of Y Garn.

4 CWM DUDODYN PATH

A steep, but nevertheless inviting, corrie that provides an interesting approach to the northern side of Y Garn. You can easily include Elidir Fawr in an approach via this route.

Start Nant Peris **(GR606584)**
Distance 8.2km (5 miles)
Time 3½ hours
Height gain 842m
Terrain steep pasture, steep-sided corrie, high mountain ridge, exposed col and rocky summit
Difficulty intermediate
Popularity quiet

Route From Nant Peris take the lane (opposite the post office) NE then NW to join a track. Continue generally NW along it as it climbs to the start of the Cwm Dudodyn Path. Follow the path as it zigzags up to the Afon Dudodyn. The path follows the Afon Dudodyn NE, first on the south bank then over a footbridge onto the north bank. Continue NE, ascending the length of Cwm Dudodyn. At the head of Cwm Dudodyn climb the very steep grassy slope NE to Bwlch y Brecan. Join the main ridge path and follow it S to Y Garn.

5 NORTH RIDGE OF ELIDIR FAWR

Long approach from the Deiniolen end of the range taking in a superb traverse of Elidir Fawr.

Start Talywaen **(GR594631)**
Distance 7.6km (4¾ miles)
Time 3½ hours
Height gain 820m
Terrain moorland, rocky corrie, rounded ridge, high open col, scree, narrow summit ridge, high mountain ridge and rocky summit
Difficulty easy
Popularity moderate

Route From the road take the Marchlyn Mawr access road ESE to the junction below the Marchlyn Bach Reservoir. Leave the road and ascend the ridge S to Elidir Fach. From the summit of Elidir Fach head SE and cross Bwlch Melynwyn to make a short but steep ascent to the summit ridge. Follow it round to Y Garn.

The summit from Bwlch Cywion with the north-east ridge in profile

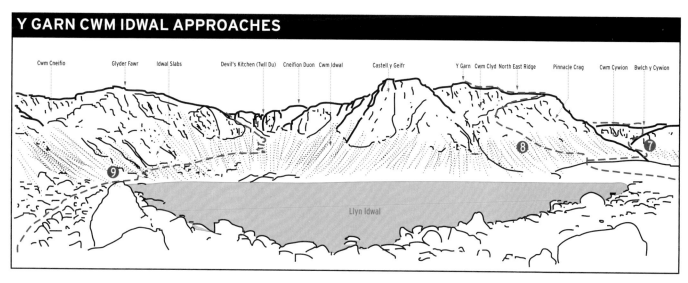

Y GARN CWM IDWAL APPROACHES

Cwm Cneifio

Glyder Fawr

Idwal Slabs

Devil's Kitchen (Twll Du)

Cneifion Duon

Cwm Idwal

Castell y Geifr

Y Garn

Cwm Clyd

North East Ridge

Pinnacle Crag

Cwm Cywion

Bwlch y Cywion

Llyn Idwal

ROUTES AND ILLUSTRATIONS
JEREMY ASHCROFT

Reed all about it! Llyn y Cwn soaks up the rays.

The Needle's Eye Arête.

6 NEEDLE'S EYE ARÊTE

A steep, exposed scramble up the rocks of Creigiau Gleision. The situations are superb and the scrambling consistently good. You will however need a head for heights as the exposure never relents.

Start old road at the south end of Nant Ffrancon **(GR641611)**
Distance 3km (2 miles)
Time 3-4 hours
Height gain 752m
Terrain steep corrie, scree, crags, steep arête, high mountain ridge and rocky summit
Difficulty strenuous (Grade 3 scramble) – rope may be required
Popularity quiet

Route From the road zigzag W up the southern flank of Cwm-coch to the base of Creigiau Gleision. Needle's Eye Arête bounds the R side of Eastern Gully and is followed onto the crest of Y Llymllwyd (for a full description see page 116). Head W along Y Llymllwyd to gain the main ridge at Bwlch y Cywion. Turn L and follow the main ridge SSW then SE to the summit of Y Garn.

7 CWM CYWION ROUTE

Gains the main ridge on the north side of Y Garn via the remote and little-visited Cwm Cywion.

Start Idwal Cottage **(GR650603)**
Distance 4.4km (2¾ miles)
Time 3 hours
Height gain 682m
Terrain broad craggy corrie, mountain lake, steep rocky slope, high open corrie, rounded mountain ridge and rocky summit
Difficulty intermediate
Popularity quiet

Route From Idwal Cottage take the Cwm Idwal path SE then SW to Llyn Idwal. Cross the footbridge at mouth of the lake and follow the vague path that snakes up to the base of the north-east ridge of Y Garn. Before you reach the base of the ridge leave the path and contour round the steep slopes NW into Cwm Cywion. Continue NW up through Cwm Cywion to Llyn Cywion then ascend the head wall, still generally NW, to Bwlch y Cywion. Cross the col and make the short descent to join the path on the SW side of Foel-goch. Turn L on the path and follow it S then SE to the summit rocks of Y Garn.

Striding out towards the summit, with Tryfan behind.

8 NORTH-EAST RIDGE

A superb knife-edge ridge which rears up steeply from the Ogwen Valley direct to Y Garn's summit rocks.

Start Idwal Cottage **(GR650603)**
Distance 3.2km (2 miles)
Time 2½ hours
Height gain 637m
Terrain broad craggy corrie, mountain lake, steep rocky slope, steep rocky ridge and rocky summit
Difficulty strenuous (Grade 1 scramble)
Popularity moderate

Route From Idwal Cottage take the Cwm Idwal path SE then SW to Llyn Idwal. Cross the footbridge at the mouth of the lake and follow the vague path that snakes up to the base of the north-east ridge. Continue along the path as it climbs the crest of the ridge SW to Y Garn's summit ridge. At the top turn L and head S to the summit rocks.

9 DEVIL'S KITCHEN PATH

The head of Cwm Idwal is ringed by a series of high, towering crags. This path takes a narrow, winding route across the flank of the darkest of these cliffs.

Start Idwal Cottage **(GR650603)**
Distance 4.4km (2¾ miles)
Time 2½ hours
Height gain 637m
Terrain broad, craggy corrie, mountain lake, moderate scree-covered slopes and rocky summit
Difficulty strenuous
Popularity busy

Route From Idwal Cottage take the Cwm Idwal path SE then SW to Llyn Idwal. Take the path on the E side of the lake and follow it S past the base of Idwal Slabs then W up the scree path towards the Devil's Kitchen. At the base of the Devil's Kitchen, among the boulders, the path swings S and climbs a vague ramp line before turning SW up an open grove. Ascend the groove to reach the broad col occupied by Llyn y Cwn. From Llyn y Cwn follow the main path NNW then NW up the summit slopes to the top of Y Garn.

"I've climbed it"

Sarah Edgar, Caernarfon

Our friend Dave had offered to get me and Sally up the 14 3000ers over three months before we reached our 50th birthdays, and today was supposed to be a quick up and down Elidir Fawr from Nant Peris on a grey September day.

When we got to the top of Elidir Fawr, we were wet and knackered. Sally peered through the cloud at Y Garn and said, "If that's another 3000er we might as well do it now, because I'm not bloody coming up here again!" The clouds lifted as we set off and we were soon sat on the summit of Y Garn with the most spectacular view over Cwm Idwal to the Glyders, Tryfan and the Carneddau. Even Sally was smiling!

Nick Coates, Leeds

It was one of those days we all long for – blue skies, clear air and snowy summits. My mate Rob and I were students at Bangor, allowing us easy and all-too-tempting access to the delights of Snowdonia. Very soon, guilty thoughts disappeared at the sight of the bulk of Y Garn. The weather was grand, the company was great, and the climbing and views spectacular.

We scrambled up the east ridge, and there it was, the summit, beckoning us. It was magical, not only the fact that we had the mountain to ourselves, but the even sweeter thought that we were missing the delights of lectures.

Mike Doolan, Leominster

I set off to climb Y Garn in winter (many years ago!) on my old Yamaha 70cc motorcycle, and on arriving at Oggie Cottage, I almost fell off the bike in my frozen state! Some 24 years later, I still visit Snowdonia at least once a year, and my children know all about Dad's first climb on Y Garn!

On the face of things, Britain has little to offer the modern-day Shackleton or Thesiger. There's a distinct lack of empty quarters, untraversed mountain ranges and forbidden cities. But you don't have to travel halfway round the world to find adventure. Even in the most popular mountain areas of the UK you can ditch the car, avoid the honeypots, and best of all, you don't need canoes, herds of llamas or waterproof underpants to do it. I'd planned a Snowdonia trip with Tom and Steph, hoping to discover the quiet side of three north Wales mountains – Cadair Idris, the Rhinogs and Snowdon – a weekend expedition crossing Snowdonia by bike and boot.

The Kings Youth Hostel, tucked into a wooded valley to the north-west of Cadair Idris, is the perfect base camp from which to launch a weekend expedition. From the rambling hostel, set by a stone bridge over a sparkling river, a narrow lane twists and winds to Cadair Idris. With its ancient Lost World plateau, this mountain hovers uncertainly on the southern limits of the Snowdonia National Park. Well might it, says Bry Lynas, author of *Snowdonia Rocky Rambles*. Strictly speaking, Cadair Idris has no claim to the name of Snowdonia, being part of a separate, more ancient mountain architecture. The volcanic rocks that jut and carve around Cadair Idris' dramatic cliffs and lonely corries are even older than those of the Snowdon massif; but what difference does a few million years here or there make? As far as the National Parks are concerned, Cadair Idris is part of Snowdonia.

Being both striking and accessible, Cadair Idris has long been popular with walkers and climbers. For adventurous walkers, the ridges and corries invite exploration; and the Cwryfry arête, which seems to pour down in an almost unbroken arc from the summit of the mountain to the tarn, Llyn y Gadair, is a highly rated climb. Aside from these attentions, it has drawn many admirers over the years. The Victorians, strange folk that they were, paid tribute to its wild beauty in their own idiosyncratic way. This took the form of building a pony track to the summit and a refreshment hut to sit in and take tea or opium, or whatever it was that the odd buggers did when they took it into their heads to climb mountains. Cadair Idris continues to attract every kind of mystic and Harry Potter wannabe, drawn perhaps by the story that anyone who spends a night on the summit awakes either a madman or a poet. Myth and legend cling gently to this mountain, rather like the fine summer mist that descended on us as we climbed up the Foxes Path, a rougher alternative to the north of the well-trodden Pony Path.

Shhh! Snowdonia on the quiet

USING BOOTS AND BIKES TO BREAK AWAY FROM THE MOST POPULAR PATHS, TRAIL JOINS THE HUSH-HOUR TRAFFIC IN NORTH WALES.

Words **Maria del Carmen Clegg**
Photography **Matthew Roberts**

Snowdon, Craig-ddu and
Y Lliwedd from the peaceful
Watkin Path.

151

On a clear day, the view from this summit is said to be one of the most spectacular in Wales: a vast panorama of valleys and lakes, summits, estuary and sea to distract you from the steep climb you've just toiled up. We piled our 'sacks against an outside wall of the ruined Victorian hut and sat down to eat lunch. An optimistic gull swooped low through the mists to join us, reminding us that even if we couldn't see the sea, it was close enough for this feathered opportunist to pay us a visit.

Through the mists we explored the eerie crags until we picked up Cadair Idris' most popular track – the Pony Path – down to the valley and the remnants of ancient woodland. Twisted oaks towered protectively over stripling rowans, and mossy boulders hid tiny woodland flowers. All around, the air bustled with birds and insects; while, ahead of us, wheatears disappeared into the trees with a flash of white tail feathers. Victorian prudery being what it was led to the renaming of the white-arse as the wheatear. Tom was amazed to see a ring ouzel, the publicity-shy mountain blackbird that you'll often hear singing, but whose black

A fleeting glimpse of Cadair Idris' Cyfrwy arête.

plumage and thick white neckstripe you'll rarely see. We then spotted a second one, and the four of us stood still to watch it sing until it flew away. Cadair Idris' rugged mountain wilderness could really bring out your inner twitcher…

We piled into the pub, looking forward to planning the next stage of our trip over something with chips. A well-meaning friend had said to me, "You've got to go to this fantastic pub under Cadair Idris; they have two enormous owls that sit and glare at you while you eat." Well, the owls were elsewhere, but the bar staff were doing a fine job in their absence. The mention of the word 'bikes' over our unfolded map sent the barman into an unprovoked spitting rage of howling indignation.

"You'd better not be riding on footpaths!" he cried, and glared at us even more darkly than he had before. Wondering if it was something we'd said, I tried to smooth over fraught rural relations with the other barman, who'd seemed a bit friendlier. Well, at least a little less openly hostile...

"So, do you get many walkers round here?" I offered, leaning on the bar, and trying just that little bit too hard to be nice.

"Walkers!" he sneered, "Oh yes, we get plenty of walkers. But *they're* the worst," he muttered darkly, nodding at a harmless-looking bunch of elderly daytrippers innocently tucking into gammon and pineapple in the snug, and unaware of the contempt being heaped on them. I picked up my food order – battered olive branch – and retreated to the table where my companions were still undecided whether to laugh or leave.

There's a rich irony in these antediluvian attitudes to bikes and boots. Last year, the Wales Tourist Board launched a new website to showcase the energetic efforts of the knobbly tyre lobby. Joint projects with Forest Enterprise have led to the opening of dedicated mountain bike areas in six prime sites in north and mid-Wales, graded like ski slopes for everything from family-friendly riding through to hand-built technical singletrack loops for the dedicated downhiller. Whether the grumpy bar stewards at the Gwernan Lake Hotel like it or not, Wales is building a reputation with the cog-noscenti as one of the most bike-friendly nations in the world.

Fed and watered, and back at base camp, we set our sights on Tal-y-bont. The area's well-served by the National Cycle Network, following quiet lanes and dedicated trails across the Mawddach estuary, through the pretty fishing town of Barmouth towards Tal-y-bont and Penrhyndeudaeth and Garreg. Here the NCN splits off east and west: east towards the Vale of Ffestiniog, and west towards Caernarfon and the coast. But if you'd rather save your energies for walking, or if you get caught out by bad weather, there are good rail links along the coast.

Cycling across the old railway bridge at Barmouth, we looked back to see the summit of Cadair Idris, free of cloud in the afternoon heat. The warm breeze picked up fine grains of sand and blew gently into our faces like a mild case of pins and needles. Meanwhile at the end of the arrow-straight bridge, Barmouth village tempted us with seaside promises. I stopped to chat to Karen, who takes the £1.20 toll for the footbridge. Every morning, she steps out of her house and walks next door to the swingbridge toll booth that's been her office for almost 20 years.

"You couldn't have a better view," Karen says, as I take in the scene. "Every day I sit here, and see the estuary filling up, watch the tides coming in and out, and see the weather over the mountains." Even more remarkably, her grandmother before her had the same job for 30 years before retiring.

"Every day, I watch the tides coming in and out, and see the weather over the mountains..."

KAREN, TOLLKEEPER, BARMOUTH BRIDGE

"When I was a little girl, I used to play between the turnstile and the gate. I never dreamed I'd end up working here! It's such a nice area to live." Does she think her children will take over from her when she retires? "I've got a granddaughter, but I'd rather she went to university. It's no job for a young person; it's a way of life." In her little booth, Karen also works as a one-woman visitor centre, and pulls out a bundle of sepia photos to explain the history of the railway bridge and the town. We reluctantly leave the peaceful estuary behind to contine north to Tal-y-bont.

This was to be our next base for exploring the Rhinogs, a craggy crinkle in the bulging mass of mountains between the Glaslyn and Mawddach estuaries known as the Harlech Dome. Rhinog Fawr and Rhinog Fach are armour-clad with boulder fields, unstable scree slopes and rampant heather, giving them a reputation for being extraordinarily rough walking country. But these peaks are poorly served by bridleways so if you're biking, the best tracks cut across the high ground. These inland weaknesses in the mountains' defences were probably the easiest way of transporting goods across the river before the Barmouth bridge was built.

A stiff uphill ride out of Tal-y-bont flushed our legs into action, and in just a few miles it seemed as though we'd left the coast a long way behind, and were cycling into the heart of wild Wales.

Of course, bikes are wonderful machines but there's one major problem with them. The paranoia. Bikes are

Biking into the Rhinogs from Tal-y-bont, not a soul for miles.

Steph pulls off the 'effortless cool' look.

nickable, because they're a) expensive b) desirable and c) they have the major design flaw of being both loot and getaway vehicle. Combining biking and walking has been popular for years among Munro-baggers and winter climbers who use them to shorten a walk-in, or take advantage of the time saved to squeeze in one more route.

In the wilds of Scotland, your bike will likely remain unmolested while you're in the hills; but in popular areas you do need to be a bit more careful. I've heard of tales of people carrying camouflage nets to cover their bikes; however, you can improvise. In the height of summer, bracken or a patch of woodland can easily conceal a couple of bikes. However, in a broad valley, with four frames painted in such sizzling colours that they were probably visible from space, we were wishing we'd raided the army surplus store.

I'd already seen a patch of plantation marked on the map that we could head for if we had to, but Tom and Steph were clearly experts in the art of the cycle stash. We carried the bikes away from the path, dropping over a hummock to hide them between a drystone wall and some waist-high bracken. It wasn't until we'd locked the bikes together and put our boots on that we almost tripped over the ribcage of an unlucky sheep. The perfect camouflage! Hmm, perhaps not ...

Diffwys is one of the rare mountains with a bridleway that goes all the way to the top. That's not to say that you'd enjoy riding it; just that you can. The terrain leading up to the two highest peaks in the Rhinogs – Y Llethr at 2,480 feet, and Diffwys at 2,460 feet – is

The day's end, in a spectacularly empty Cwm Llan.

Airy, not scary: Snowdon's south ridge, Bwlch Main.

A welcome stop on a hot summer day.

easier underfoot than on the more northerly peaks; and, because there's a good network of byways and bridleways, you can play around with the amount of biking you want to do, and either cross the range over Braich, or just use the bikes to get close to Diffwys and Y Llethr. Even so, arm yourself with information on what's rideable, and what's a 'carry'. Pop into a local bike shop to buy a couple of spare inner tubes, and most people will be happy to help.

We traversed the skyline ridge on foot to take in the two highest points of the range, and traced the shape of a badly buckled wheel rim to drop back down to our hidden treasure. How many times have you looked at a long, flat farm track, with the best of the day already etched in your mind, and thought, 'This would be so good on a bike...'? Well, this was a dream come true. Jumping back on our bikes, too hill-weary to bother changing our shoes, we freewheeled all the way back to Tal-y-bont. Balancing walking boots on clip-in pedals, we flew down the open track that would have taken us another 45 minutes to walk, rolling into base camp on a tidal wave of feel-good endorphins that carried us the 15 miles to our bed for the night at Bryn Gwynant Youth Hostel.

The National Cycle Network doesn't quite link up with Snowdon from the south, but it's still possible to follow quiet-ish roads to the start of your favourite route to Wales' highest peak.

There are several bridleways leading to the summit of Snowdon but again, you probably wouldn't want to ride most of them, unless you're like the legendary eccentric Nicholas Crane, who took a mountain bike along Crib Goch. He was photographed teetering along the precarious ridge (and riding a fine legal line too, as it doesn't really have mountain bike access). To avoid conflict with walkers (and also presumably to save Mr Crane from doing himself an injury) a voluntary agreement has been reached between the National Park and mountain bikers. This allows cyclists access to Snowdon's bridleways at any time during the winter months, and before 10am and after 5pm from May to September. If you want to cycle to the summit of Snowdon, the best approach is from Llanberis, following the railway line. And no, you can't catch the train up and bike down!

The next day, we're far too relaxed to cycle up the Watkin path at 5 in the morning so that we can ride down before 10. Instead, it's a leisurely breakfast and a straightforward stroll up. Apart from anything else, it means that we can leave all the paraphernalia of biking at the hostel. Most of the half million people who tread the summit of Snowdon every year pile up from the Llanberis valley by train and tourist track, so this side of the mountain is remarkably peaceful. The Watkin Path passes ruined copper mines and settlements, and is easily the most rugged path to the top – far more wild and picturesque than the Pig Track, and quieter than the equally dramatic Snowdon Ranger which leads directly up from the Youth Hostel and the Llanberis path. If you can live without tagging the top then you don't even have to see the summit caff; you can just follow the exposed Bwlch Main to the slender ridge that links Snowdon and Yr Aran and make believe that Snowdon's still a wilderness. The only really essential ingredient in a weekend expedition is your imagination.

The Youth Hostel at Bryn Gwynant with views over Llyn Gwynant. Call 0870 870 8808 for YHA membership and hostel details; www.yha.org.uk

Boots into bikes will go! For inspiration on other suitable bike-hikes, see *Mountain bike guide: North Wales* by Pete Burnsall, pb Ernest Press.

Rights to ride

Most mountain bikers aspire to big days out in real mountains, and the excellent rights of way system in England and Wales makes it possible to take your bike to many upland areas. However, with rights come responsibilities. The main contentions are bikes being where they shouldn't be, or riding too fast and too close to other hill users. The following guidelines should help to make yours and everybody else's day out more enjoyable.

Where to ride

Throughout England and Wales, cyclists have a right of passage on bridleways, RUPPs, BOATs and some unclassified county roads (UCRs). These are all marked on OS maps. Never ride on footpaths, and don't assume you can ride the tracks and trails that cross 'open access' ground (usually shown as dotted or dashed black lines on maps). These are usually tracks that exist on the ground, but do not always carry a right of way. De facto access may apply only to people on foot. For hassle-free riding, visit one of the dedicated mountain bike centres, such as those at Coed y Brenin and Afan Argoed Forest Park – tel. 08701 211251 (Visit Wales); details also at www.mbwales.com, or investigate waymarked trails around towns such as Betws-y-coed, Machynlleth and Llanwrtyd Wells. Info on the National Cycle Network is available from Sustrans – tel. (0117) 929 0888; www.sustrans.org.

How to ride

Legally, cyclists should give way to walkers and horses; but, in practice, a courteous manner usually leaves everybody happy. When approaching other hill users who have seen you, slow down. If you really want to ride a section at your own pace, stop and wait for them to pass. Never speed past a horse or a group of walkers. As well as frightening the people, who may not realise that you are in control, you could easily make a horse bolt. Remember that dogs are often unseen, sniffing around in the bushes, and will run out if they hear you. Most dogs have little road sense, and are irresistibly drawn towards bikes.

If you are approaching others from behind and haven't been seen yet, again slow down but this time call out a polite hello well before you pass. This will warn them that you are there, and show that you are human. Get a bell: it usually raises a smile, but it's no substitute for a cheerful greeting. Often walkers or riders will stand back and hold onto their dog to allow you to pass safely. It sounds obvious, but it's important to thank them. A smile and a few polite words go a long way. Also, remember that if you're wearing a helmet and sunglasses, you can actually look quite intimidating.

Ride popular trails like Loughrigg Terrace in the Lakes, or Mam Tor in the Peaks, mid-week when it's quiet. If you can't take the odd day off then try an early start or a late finish. It's better to avoid these places during peak holiday seasons.

Some rights of way pass through farmyards, courtyards or even gardens. Walk rather than ride through these, as kids may be playing nearby and the family cat may be sunning itself in the road around the next blind bend.

Finally, you'll have heard people complaining that mountain bikes cause excessive erosion. This is definitely a matter for debate but your riding style can be adapted to minimise damage to the mountain environment. Wherever possible, ride on hard-packed trails, particularly when the ground is wet. It's no fun slogging over boggy moorland, and your tyre tracks will cause drainage gullies that could turn into a small stream with the next rainstorm. If you're on a trail with wet or boggy patches, ride or carry the bike straight through. Don't be tempted to ride or walk around them as you'll only widen the boggy area, and in the long term the precious singletrack will start to resemble the M5. Where possible, save soft springy moorland crossings for drier spells. The most obvious sign that irresponsible riders have used a trail are long skid marks into gates or sharp bends. These are easily avoided; apply the brakes earlier and more smoothly. Skids are for kids!

Bikes and Snowdon

Snowdonia National Park Authority has written a leaflet on the National Voluntary Cycling Agreement – tel. (01766) 770274. The agreement has opened up more routes for bikers, including the quarry track to the Watkin Path as far as the ruined coppermines by the Gladstone Rock. Bike up to here for an excellent start and finish to the stunning Watkin Path / Snowdon summit / south ridge circuit.

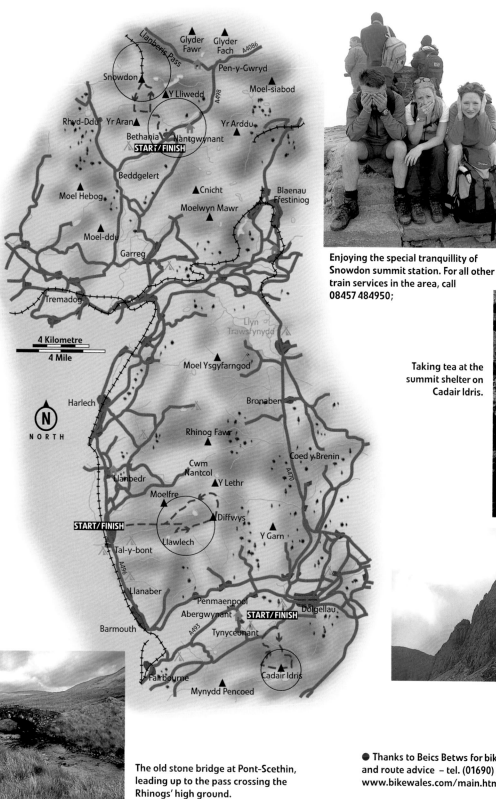

Enjoying the special tranquillity of Snowdon summit station. For all other train services in the area, call 08457 484950;

The Gladstone Rock commemorates the official opening of the Watkin Path in 1892 by prime minister William Gladstone, then aged 83. From *The complete guide to Snowdon* by Robert Jones, pb Gwasg Carreg Gwalch.

Taking tea at the summit shelter on Cadair Idris.

The Cyfrwy arête, a classic Grade 3S scramble/Difficult climb. *Classic Mountain Scrambles in England and Wales* by Graham Thompson; *The Long Routes*, by Robin Ashcroft, pb Mainstream.

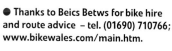

The old stone bridge at Pont-Scethin, leading up to the pass crossing the Rhinogs' high ground.

● Thanks to Beics Betws for bike hire and route advice – tel. (01690) 710766; www.bikewales.com/main.htm.